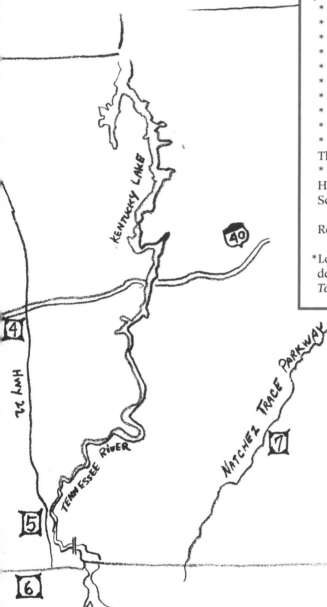

8) Jackson
  * Gold Find
  * Riverside Cemetery
  * First National Bank
  * Alexandria
  * Butler Race Track
  * Hanging Gallows
  * Casey Jones Village
  * Casey Jones Grave
  * Johnson Street Cemetery
  * Lancaster Park
  The Grove
  * Camp Beauregard
  Highland Park
  Southern Engine and
    Boiler Works
  Rothrock Stadium

*Locations of places
described in
Tales of Madison.

Old Trails and Tales of
TENNESSEE

Old Trails and Tales of
TENNESSEE

For Pam

Travel with me down the old paths and rivers where Crockett and Jackson once walked!.

Harbert Alexander
November 11, 2004

Harbert Alexander

Illustrated by Richard Brown

It was a pleasure working with Harbert —
Dick Brown

Old Trails and Tales of
TENNESSEE

Published by Harbert Alexander

Library of Congress Control Number: 2004092856
ISBN: 0-9753737-0-6

Cover and Text Illustrations by Richard Brown

Edited, Designed, and Manufactured by
Favorite Recipes® Press
An imprint of

P.O. Box 305142
Nashville, Tennessee 37230
800-358-0560

Art Director: Steve Newman
Book Design: Bruce Gore
Project Editor: Linda Jones

Manufactured in the United States of America
First Printing: 2004
2,500 copies

Introduction and Acknowledgments

Long ago, a very long time ago, at the end of the Ice Age, the first animals began appearing in North America. The animal life of that time included many types of large animals that are now extinct. They included mammoths and mastodons, wild horses, camels, bison, and saber-toothed tigers. As they moved through the land, they made trails. As the Native Americans appeared, they followed the animals, hunting them along the trails the animals had created. These animal trails would become the first roads.

History is found along the old roads and trails. That is where the people were who made the history. As they migrated across the face of America, in what historians call "Manifest Destiny," they followed the roads. Pioneers, settlers, soldiers, robbers, and thieves all followed the roads.

Some would travel a different type of road, one made of water. They came down the streams and rivers in everything that would float, from canoes to steamboats. This flood of people crossing the land reminds me of rainfall gathering on a window. Suddenly, one drop will seem to explode and travel across the window. This is what our forefathers did as they came along the old roads, whether dirt or water, on their way across America, creating history as they went.

Come with me along the old trails. Our history is all around us—if we only look! Perhaps you will recognize or remember some of the stories. Many of them will be new to you.

Come with me to Randolph, a city that no longer exists, or saddle up with David Crockett as he leaves Tennessee for Texas. Watch our young men go off to war, from the Civil War to the war in Iraq. Get to know the young German soldiers, recently with Rommel in North Africa, and now prisoners-of-war in West Tennessee. Follow the soldiers and returning boatmen along the Natchez Trace, or experience the horrors of the yellow fever epidemics of the 1880s. Tennessee has a wonderful history—it is ours to enjoy and experience again and again.

My thanks and gratitude to the many historians who encouraged and helped me with this book. Bob Bond introduced me to Obadiah Dodson and gave me the history of Woodland Church. Joe Thornton helped to put the story of Tabernacle and the early Methodists together. Jonathan Smith, always my most reliable resource, kept me straight on David Crockett and his home place near Rutherford. Reese Moses, in the Brownsville Library, gave me her files on Richard Halliburton, and Faye Davidson in Bolivar helped me to put the Edison story together. Joe B. Guinn of Memphis led me to Randolph and climbed down in the old Confederate powder magazine with me.

Pictures make the story, and Dick Brown makes my stories come alive with his illustrations. Look at the pictures he did of Richard Halliburton's China Junk or the picture of the *Sultana*. How fortunate I am to have him as my partner.

Most of all, I appreciate the support of my best friend, my wife, who encouraged me and traveled with me from Elmwood to Tabernacle, from the Memphis Library to Shiloh. She was always there to encourage and support me.

Martha Peddy proofread all of the stories and helped with rules of punctuation and capitalization—rules I learned in high school and forgot long ago. And as always, my associate, Regina Barnhill, typed every story. This book would not have been possible without her. And, even better, she liked what I wrote!

Table of Contents

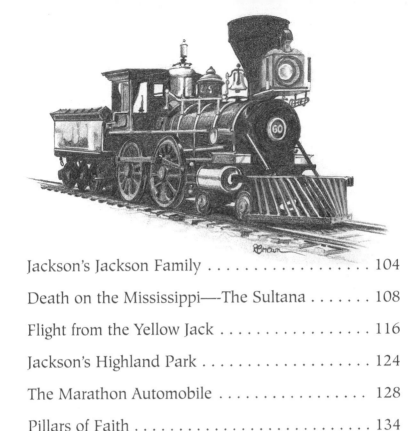

Wooly Mammoth

Was That a Panther?

Two years ago, a friend of mine was sitting in his truck on a construction site just outside of Jackson. It was mid-morning on a hot summer day when he saw a large jet-black cat with a long tail come out of the swamp and go into a cotton field. The individual who saw this animal is an experienced hunter who spends much of his time in the field. He is quick to tell you that he knows what a panther looks like, and that is what he saw. Yet we all know that panthers no longer live in West Tennessee. What he saw that day remains a mystery. However, panthers once lived here. As our environment changes, so does the wildlife around us.

When the first Native Americans came into West Tennessee some 10,000 years ago, large forests of pine, hemlock, oak, hickory, and chestnut flourished in a climate that was somewhat cooler and damper than it is today. The animal life of those times included many large species that are now extinct. Among those animals were mammoths, mastodons, saber-toothed tigers, giant ground sloths, wild horses and camels, and straight-horned bison.

By the time the first settlers came into West Tennessee in the 1820s, all of these animals had long disappeared, but new ones had taken their place. One of the best descriptions of early settlers in West Tennessee is found in a book entitled *Old Times in West Tennessee*. The book describes the Joseph Williams family and their journey of 300 miles in covered wagon from Mississippi through the Choctaw and Chickasaw country to Tipton County on a creek near the Hatchie River. The week before Christmas, they killed six bears, twelve wild turkeys, and one panther. After skinning the bears, they had more than 2,000 pounds of meat!

As settlers moved into West Tennessee, the habitat began to change. As forests were cleared and fields of cotton and corn were planted, the animals were pushed deeper into the woods. Hunting pressure also increased as pioneers depended on hunting to feed their families. The big animals were the first to disappear. Buffalo were last seen in Kentucky in 1780, and by 1800, they were gone from Tennessee. The last elk was killed in Obion County in 1896. The last bear in Haywood County was killed in 1865. Thirty years later, the last West Tennessee bear was killed in Lauderdale County.

Cougars (or panthers, as they are called) and wolves disappeared before the 1900s. Flocks of passenger pigeons used to number in the millions. Loss of habitat and hunting pressure caused them to begin to decline in the 1850s. By 1914, they were extinct.

And yet there are many good things happening around us, thanks to conservation efforts and habitat preservation and restoration. Elk have been restocked in East Tennessee. Thanks to the Tennessee Wildlife Resources Agency, there are more deer and turkeys now than when the first settlers arrived. Coyotes came into West Tennessee in the 1970s for the first time. And in the last year or so, hunters and farmers have begun seeing armadillos. They are here for the first time, too.

Who knows what will come next? Foxes, skunks, raccoons, and possums have moved into our city limits. Keep your eyes open the next time you go into the woods. Who knows, you might see a panther!

Dr. William E. Butler

Man of the Year

For many years, the Jackson Exchange Club has chosen a Man of the Year. To be so selected is a high honor for the individual who receives it. In 1992, when I was chosen, I considered it the high point of my years in Jackson.

Yet long ago, there was an individual whose accomplishments were far beyond any of the modern recipients. He was a doctor, philanthropist, soldier, and farmer. His name was Dr. William E. Butler. He is often called the Father of Jackson. Consider his life.

The son of a Revolutionary War soldier, he was born in Carlisle, Pennsylvania, in 1789. After graduating with a degree in medicine from the University of Pennsylvania, he moved to Murfreesboro. In 1813, he married Martha (Patsy) Thompson Hays, niece of Andrew Jackson.

During the War of 1812, Dr. Butler joined the staff of Colonel Thomas Hart Benton of the Second Regiment of Infantry under General Andrew Jackson and was present with them at the Battle of New Orleans, serving as Jackson's surgeon general. Following the War of 1812, Butler was with Jackson in two campaigns against the Creek Indians.

Butler was one of the first white men to come into West Tennessee following the treaty with the Chickasaw Indians in 1818, accompanying James Caruthers on a trip down the Forked Deer in 1819. Apparently, he liked what he found, for he returned two years later with his family. But getting to Jackson was no easy affair. Loading his family and all of their furniture on a flatboat, he floated down the Cumberland to the Ohio, then down the Mississippi to the Forked Deer, where they poled it up to a site in Jackson near the present-day jail. On this site, he built a double log house on a 640-acre tract. In 1821, he planted his first crop of cotton and erected a cotton gin that he had brought from Davidson County.

The following year, Dr. Butler, along with two associates, donated thirty acres of land for the establishment of the town of Alexandria (renamed Jackson in August of that year). This land, along with twenty-four acres purchased from Thomas Shannon, is the site of Jackson's downtown area. Following the establishment of Jackson as county seat, Butler was appointed as a commissioner for the town.

Besides his activities in getting the young town started, Butler seemed to be involved in everything else connected with Jackson. He was an elder in the Presbyterian Church, serving also on the first building committee in the early 1830s. Apparently, he switched over to the Episcopalians, for he signed the articles of association to begin St. Luke's Parish in 1832.

On a site where today's Chamber of Commerce building is located, Butler had a racetrack that Andrew Jackson and his wife, Rachel, visited in 1825. In 1843, Butler donated this land to a school for young ladies named Memphis Conference Female Institute. Eighty years later, this school moved to its present site and is now known as Lambuth University. Butler also gave the land for the old Mobile and Ohio railroad shops on Chester Street.

By 1825, Butler was a member of the county court and served on the Board of Trustees of the Jackson Male Academy. He also served as an agent for the State Bank.

In later years, Dr. Butler built a fine large brick home on Royal Street in Jackson. The spacious banquet table was made to seat thirty guests. Beautiful furniture and rugs were in the house, and oil paintings of the doctor and his wife as well as a number of steel engravings were on the walls.

David Crockett was elected to the state legislature in 1821, representing Middle Tennessee. In 1823, he moved to Carroll County on the Rutherford Fork of the Obion River. During the winter, his only income came from selling bear and deer meat or collecting a three-dollar bounty on wolf hides. To collect his money, he had to travel to Jackson, forty miles to the south.

On a February trip to Jackson, he spent an evening in a tavern sharing drinks (or horns, as they were called) with Dr. Butler and two other local politicians, Joseph Lynn and Duncan McIver. Each of these three planned to seek a seat in the legislature for the newly formed Madison County. (There was only one seat.) Since all three of them were candidates, they jokingly suggested that Crockett should run as well. As he lived more than two hours from Jackson, he dismissed the idea as preposterous. Several weeks later, a neighbor showed Crockett a copy of a newspaper, *The Jackson Pioneer*, listing him as a candidate. Whether it was an accident or a joke will never be known. (Some think Crockett put it in the paper himself, but was unwilling to tell his wife, Elizabeth, he would be gone from home for long periods of time politicking.) At any rate, Crockett told his wife that he would make whoever was responsible pay for the prank. He declared he would go to Jackson and win the election, thus defending his honor.

Crockett's three opponents soon agreed that only Butler should oppose Crockett. This selection of Butler to oppose Crockett occurred because of Dr. Butler's marriage to Andrew Jackson's niece, and also because he was considered to be the most clever of the three.

As the campaign began for the seat to represent Madison County in the state legislature, Crockett was at a disadvantage in that Dr. Butler was well known and he was not. His colorful nature helped him overcome this quickly. In his autobiography,

Crockett wrote, "I hadn't been out long before I found the people began to talk about the bear hunter, the man from the cane."

At a campaign meeting held by Colonel Adam Alexander, who was running for the United States Congress, Crockett and Butler traded good-natured insults. At this point, Davy explained how he planned to win the election:

"I told him that when I set out electioneering, I would go prepared to put every man on as good footing when I left him as I found him on. I would therefore have me a large buckskin hunting-shirt made, with a couple of pockets holding about a peck each; and that in one I would carry a great big twist of tobacco, and in the other my bottle of liquor; for I knowed when I met a man and offered him a dram, he would throw out his quid of tobacco to take one, and after he had taken his horn, I would out with my twist and give him another chaw. And in this way he would not be worse off than when I found him; and I would be sure to leave him in a first-rate good humour. He said I could beat him electioneering all hollow. I told him I would give him better evidence of that before August, notwithstanding he had many advantages over me. And particularly in the way of money; but I told him that I would go on the products of the country; that I had industrious children, and the best coon dogs, and they would hunt every night till midnight to support my election; and when the coon fur wa'nt good, I would myself go a wolfing, and shoot down a wolf, and skin his head,

and his scalp would be good to me for three dollars, in our state treasury money; and in this way I would get along on the big string. He stood like he was both amused and astonished, and the whole crowd was in a roar of laughter."

Once the election began in earnest, Crockett aimed more of his tricks at Butler. When the doctor invited Davy to his home for dinner after one of their debates, Crockett made a big point of not stepping on any of the fine rugs throughout the house. To avoid doing so, he jumped over them, even managing to leap into his chair at dinner, and kept his feet on the chair rungs rather than letting them touch the carpet. At their next debate, Crockett told his listeners that Butler had finer materials in the carpets on his floor than their wives and children had on their backs. This dinner took place at Butler's first residence, the double log cabin near Riverside. Years later, he built the fine large brick home with the banquet table large enough to seat thirty people. And even though Crockett was long dead, the Butlers were still thought of as living like royalty because they had carpets on their floors. Thus, the street where he built the new house was named Royal and is Jackson's Royal Street of today!

Perhaps Crockett's best trick came at a later debate toward the end of the campaign. Both candidates gave virtually the same speech time after time. Dr. Butler made the mistake of allowing Davy to speak first. Taking advantage of his keen ear for mimicry and his retentive memory, Davy gave the doctor's speech almost word for word, leaving the doctor speechless. Butler soon recovered and gave a different speech.

Throughout this and later campaigns, Crockett would try to speak last. If Butler had spoken for a long time, Crockett would give a much shorter response—usually just a joke—and then offer to treat the crowd to a drink at the bar. Nothing could have been more popular to a frontier audience.

Late in the campaign, two other candidates entered the race. This proved to be an advantage for Crockett as they only took votes away from Butler. When election day came, the voters responded to one of their own rather than the aristocratic Dr. Butler, and Crockett won by almost 250 votes.

Though Butler lost the election, he had his revenge in later years, when he helped to place the whole Andrew Jackson political machine behind Adam Huntsman. When Crockett lost the election to Huntsman, he headed west to Texas and his final destiny at the Alamo. Butler lived out his life in Jackson, continuing to be involved in everything around him. He died in 1882 at the age of 93.

Milton Brown

The Man Who Voted for Texas

There is a popular expression that says, "If it weren't for Tennessee, there wouldn't be a Texas." Though the expression is overused, there is much truth in it, especially since so many Tennesseans joined in the fight for Texas' independence from Mexico. One individual from Jackson, though not a soldier, played a key role in Texas becoming the twenty-eighth state to be admitted to the Union in 1845. His name was Milton Brown.

Born in Lebanon, Ohio, in 1804, he moved to Nashville when he was nineteen to study law in the office of Felix Grundy, a brilliant criminal lawyer and Democratic leader. Leaving Nashville, he practiced law in Paris, Tennessee, for a short time before moving his law practice to Jackson in 1832.

In 1834, he was appointed to defend John Murrell, the most infamous criminal in Jackson's history. Most people anticipated that Murrell would be hung for murder if convicted and advised Brown that accepting the assignment could ruin his career. Brown took the case and succeeded in a reprieve from the death sentence for his client, even though he was convicted on a lesser charge of stealing slaves. This case enhanced his reputation as one of the best lawyers in the state. In addition to his growing reputation as an attorney, Brown had become one of the leading debaters of West Tennessee, speaking out frequently at political rallies and Fourth of July celebrations.

In 1837, he was appointed by the Governor as Chancellor of West Tennessee. In 1839, he resigned as Chancellor to run as a Whig nominee for the U.S. House of Representatives, to which he was elected. Brown continued in this position for eight years, emerging in Congress as a leader of the Southern Whigs, known for constantly attacking Democratic leaders in Congress as well as in Tennessee. In 1843, he entered into a colorful debate in Jackson with James K. Polk two years before Polk was elected President.

More than anything else, Brown is remembered for his deadlock-breaking resolution to admit Texas to the Union. Various bills to do so had failed, and it appeared that their admission as a new state would fail, were it not for Brown's efforts to reach a compromise between the Whigs and Democrats.

After leaving Congress in 1847, he was urged to seek a position on the Tennessee Supreme Court or to run for the United States Senate. Declining these offers, he turned to his passion for promoting railroads. From 1854 to 1856, he was president of the Mississippi Central and Tennessee Railroad. From 1856 to 1871, he was the first president of the board of directors of the Gulf Mobile and Ohio line (GM & O). So popular was Milton Brown that the first train into Jackson in September of 1857 had his name in large gilt letters on both sides of the engine. Milton Brown is more responsible than anyone else for covering West Tennessee with railroad lines.

No individual in Jackson's early history did more for education. When the Jackson Male Academy (now Union University) was chartered in 1834, Brown was one of the first trustees. He donated the money to build the west wing of the Memphis Conference Female Institute (now Lambuth University).

Brown was one of Tennessee's greatest Methodist lay leaders and supported the building of the First Methodist Church in Jackson. Further, he helped to organize the CME Church and Lane College.

Instrumental in plans to create an even larger university, Brown helped to found Vanderbilt University and served on its Board of Trustees until his death.

Having become one of the wealthiest men in Tennessee, he died in 1883 and is buried in Riverside Cemetery in Jackson.

August 29, 1857
First Train to Arrive in Jackson, Tennessee

Early Railroad Days in West Tennessee

Railroads began in Europe as early as the mid-1500s to haul wagonloads of coal or iron ore from underground mines. The mining railroads consisted of two wooden rails that extended down into the mines. Men or horses pulled the cars. In 1804, an English inventor named Richard Trevithick built the first steam engine. The world's first public railroad was opened in England in 1825.

In 1815, John Stevens, an American engineer, obtained a charter from the state of New Jersey to build a steam-powered railroad across the state. It would be ten years before he could raise enough money to fund the project. In 1825, his steam engine made a successful run and so became the first railroad locomotive in North America.

In the 1830s, plans began to build a railroad from Mobile to the Tennessee River at Savannah and from there to the mouth of the Ohio River. This plan would take the crops of the Ohio and Tennessee valleys to Mobile rather than to New Orleans. Thus, the rivalry between Mobile and New Orleans led to the coming of the railroad to West Tennessee. Ground was broken in Mobile in October of 1849 to begin the project. Three years later, the first thirty-three miles of the track had been finished. Public land grants in Mississippi, Alabama, and Tennessee, along with the levying of special taxes to purchase stock, helped to finance the venture.

In 1852, citizens of Madison County purchased $250,000 in stock after the issue was presented to the Madison County Court and voted on by the people. Milton Brown and William H. Stephens went from place to place speaking on behalf of the railroad, to be named the Mobile and Ohio. They spoke at Huntersville and Jack's Creek in 1852 and at Denmark in 1853. A large meeting was held at the courthouse in Jackson in April of the same year, and the editors of the newspapers made a strong effort to convince the readers that the railroads should come.

After the citizens had invested in the stock, it looked for a while as if the railroad would run a mile and one-half east of Jackson. After a lengthy squabble, the matter was settled, but the work on the road was almost halted in 1855 due to the slowness of the stockholders in paying their debts. Just as the railroad seemed destined to fail, Judge Milton Brown of Jackson was elected as president of the company. A year later, the first passenger train came to Jackson from Columbus. The editor of *The Mobile Register* concluded:

"It was an occasion for much rejoicing to us to hear the snort of the iron horse, as with headlong fury, he came dashing on his way over forest and valley dragging behind him his golden train."

By 1865, at the end of the Civil War, the line was virtually destroyed. However, within a few months, Judge Brown had the trains running again. He remained as president of the railroad until 1871.

Another railroad line, the Mississippi Central and Tennessee ran from Grand Junction to Jackson. This line was an extension of the Mississippi Central Railroad. Milton Brown was a commissioner for this charter even while he continued as president of the Mobile and Ohio. Other prominent Jacksonians joining Brown included Dr. William E. Butler and Stokley Hays. As the railroad inched toward Jackson, celebrations were held along the way. Three thousand people gathered in Bolivar for speeches and a picnic dinner on September 21, 1854. Almost two years later, the tracks reached Medon.

At last, on August 29, 1857, the track was finished, and the first train came to Jackson. Robert Cartmell recorded the following in his diary:

"Went down to Mississippi railroad—the track is finished and the cars came up for the first time tonight. There was a large crowd from town and country to witness first arrival in daylight of a train of cars. I saw nothing or heard nothing on account of my old fool horse. He jumped and pitched and tried to run—a perfect fool and only real fool horse that was there— September 16, 1857. Today devoted to celebrating the arrival of the cars on the Mississippi Central and Tennessee Railroad. A barbecue was prepared, speeches made, cannons fired at night, fire works, balloon raising and a party—the whole passed off finely without any accident. A large number of strangers from adjoining counties and Mississippi were present. There were perhaps four thousand persons present, some said eight or ten thousand."

Though most people were excited over the coming of the railroad, some were not. Not long after the road was finished between Corinth and Jackson, a cow belonging to a Mrs. Walsh who lived just south of Henderson was killed by one of these new "iron horses." When the road did not pay damages promptly, she took the tallow from the said cow and put it on the track each day so that the train had to stop. The track had to be sanded in order to pull a grade just south of Henderson.

The railroads brought a new era to Jackson, though the Civil War put a temporary stop to it when General Sherman came south and tore up most of the track. Jackson was blessed that the railroads came through the city. Other West Tennessee cities were not so fortunate. In *Tales of Madison,* I have written about Denmark and their railroad misfortunes. Denmark began its decline when the Mobile and Ohio and the Mississippi Central and Tennessee railroads came to Jackson and not Denmark. In 1872, the citizens subscribed $25,000 in stock for a Denmark, Brownsville, and Durhamville road. This venture failed when the road never got beyond a few hundred feet of embankment built through a field west of Brownsville. A year later, the Denmark citizens refused to invest $3,000 for the Tennessee Midland Railroad, believing it would have to come through Denmark anyway. They were wrong, and the railroad went through Mercer!

It has been 145 years since the first train whistle caused Robert Cartmell's horse to run away. In looking back, it is obvious that much of Jackson's progress was due to the presence of the railroads.

Andrew Jackson

Andrew Jackson's Two Visits to West Tennessee

In 1824, Andrew Jackson was almost elected President of the United States. Both popular but controversial, Jackson ended his military career at the age of 54. Still, people remembered him as the hero of the Battle of New Orleans. Jackson's friends in Nashville were calling for him to enter the presidential race as early as 1822. In 1823, he was elected to the United States Senate.

The presidential election of 1824 was a four-man race. The other candidates were Secretary of State John Quincy Adams, Representative Henry Clay of Kentucky, and Secretary of the Treasury William H. Crawford. Jackson proved to be the popular favorite, receiving ninety-nine electoral votes. Adams was second with eighty-four, and the other two candidates received a combined total of seventy-eight votes between them. None of the candidates had achieved a majority, however, so the election went to the House of Representatives, which voted by states. Clay supported Adams, who won the presidency with a vote of thirteen states to seven for Jackson. Adams then made Clay his Secretary of State. Jackson was furious and charged Adams and Clay with making a "corrupt bargain." It was in this atmosphere that he accepted an invitation to come to Jackson in the summer of 1825.

It was only natural that Jackson be invited to the town named for him. The town had been named Alexandria at first. However, another Tennessee town had the same name, so the name was changed to Jackson on August 17, 1822. Andrew's sister-in-law, Jane Hays, lived in Jackson and had three daughters and two sons. Thus, Jackson had three nieces and two nephews here, all of whom were instrumental in the town's development. Jackson was so popular as a frontiersman and military hero that the town could well have been named for him even if he did not have family here.

The General and his wife arrived on September 25 and remained in Jackson for six days. Upon his arrival, he was escorted into town and given a special welcome by the Masons, for the charter of Jackson Lodge No. 45 was obtained while

Jackson was Grand Master of Tennessee. In addition to receptions, dinners, and speeches, Jackson most likely watched his horses race on the track owned by Dr. William E. Butler. (Butler had served with Jackson at the Battle of New Orleans and was married to Patsy Hays, Rachel Jackson's niece.)

At a public dinner given by the townspeople, Jackson gave the following toast:

"The town of Jackson where but lately roamed wild beasts and savages: behold now the abode of civilization, refinement, and hospitality."

The visit ended on October 1, when Jackson and his party left to attend a special dinner in Paris, Tennessee. Later in 1825, Jackson resigned his seat in the Senate, feeling that his chances for winning the presidency would be enhanced if he returned to private life.

It would be fifteen years before Andrew returned to Jackson, Tennessee. He was seventy-three years old, and Rachel had been dead for twelve years due to a heart attack in December of 1828. Elected as President in 1828, he served two terms before returning to The Hermitage in 1837. His hair was now white, though he still carried himself stiffly erect. In poor health, he suffered from tuberculosis and dropsy. Before coming to Jackson, he had injured a rib on his left side.

In 1832, the Whig party began to take shape in opposing Jackson. By 1840, they appeared strong enough to elect a president. "Whiggery" seemed to be raging in Madison County, but Jackson's friends felt they could be defeated if Andrew came to a political rally. The Democratic rally was held on October 8 with more than 10,000 people in attendance. Governor James K. Polk and Felix Grundy, a United States Senator and Democratic leader, accompanied Jackson.

The crowd gathered in front of the courthouse and then proceeded to Dr. Butler's home, where the three dignitaries joined them, and then moved on to a large grove of trees on North Royal Street. Andrew spoke first. His opening remarks, though strong and to the point, reflected his awareness that this would be his last trip to Jackson.

> *"It affords me unspeakable pleasure to be able to meet you on this occasion. It is probably the last time that I shall have it in my power to exchange salutations with you—the last opportunity that I shall have to thank you personally for the many proofs you have given me of your respect for my character and services. The infirmation of age admonishes me that I cannot much longer be a partner with you in the vicissitudes of this life; and I can therefore have no other feeling when honored with the cordial welcome you have accorded me, but that which belongs to a heart full of gratitude and sincerely anxious for your happiness and prosperity individually and collectively . . . My health is too feeble to sustain me in an attempt to express fully the reflections which are excited in my mind, by the view you have taken of our public affairs at this time. I cannot forbear however a brief response to some of the topics you have touched. . . This my fellow citizens is a*

great and momentous crisis in our national affairs in which our dearest rights, as freemen are concerned. The presidential election is near at hand, which will decide the fate of our Republican system; whether it will be perpetrated on the great general principle laid down in our written Constitution or changed to a great consolidation trodden under foot, our glorious Union burst asunder and your constitutional liberty lost forever."

That Andrew had grown older was obvious. After introductory remarks, Jackson had a prepared speech that Governor Polk read for him, as evidenced by joking comments in Nashville Whig newspapers. Governor Polk spoke next for two and a half hours, and then Senator Grundy spoke for a like amount of time. (People spoke longer then!) About four in the afternoon, when the speakers were finished, everyone sat down for a barbecue dinner. A highlight of the meal was a huge ashcake*, which weighed 120 pounds, baked by "Uncle" King Anderson, a veteran of three wars. The next morning, Jackson returned to Nashville. Even though Jackson's last visit was a great success, the Whig movement was too strong. Not only did the Whig party carry Madison County, but it was able to elect William Henry Harrison as the first Whig President of the United States.

---

*Most early recipes for ashcake reflect mixing cornmeal, salt, and water and forming into cakes and placing them in hot coals and ashes—thus the term ashcake.

David Crockett

Davy Crockett could "run faster, jump higher, squat lower, dive deeper, stay under longer, and come out drier than any man in the whole country."

Crockett's Route to the Alamo

Some historians might argue that Andrew Jackson was responsible for Davy Crockett going to Texas. Others might suggest that Crockett's friend Sam Houston was partly responsible. Still others would say it was Crockett's vain desire to always be center stage that put him there. No matter who was responsible, the simple fact is that David Crockett left Tennessee in the fall of 1835, bound for Texas, and never returned.

David Crockett served in the Tennessee legislature from 1821 to 1824. He won a seat in the U.S. House of Representatives from Tennessee in 1827 and was re-elected in 1829 and 1833. In Congress, Crockett broke away from fellow Tennessean President Andrew Jackson. Consequently, Whig Party leaders began promoting Crockett as a presidential candidate for the election of 1836, hoping to unseat the Jackson Democrats. In April of 1834, Crockett toured through the North testing his chances of being elected as president. The trip took him to Baltimore, Philadelphia, Boston, and New York and included his first train ride and trip on a sailing vessel. Enthusiastic crowds greeted him at every stop with gifts and fine dinners. When Congress adjourned, Crockett went back to Baltimore for a Fourth of July celebration before returning to Tennessee. While Crockett was touring the Northeast thinking about running for president, Andrew Jackson was pushing his friends in West Tennessee to gather support for Adam Huntsman to run against Crockett in the 1835 Congressional election.

Upon returning to Tennessee, it soon became obvious that the election would be very close. Crockett never missed a barbecue, house raising, or logrolling fete. Huntsman tried to emphasize Crockett's "country bumpkin" image. On one occasion, he gave Crockett a coonskin, asking if the fur was good. David handed it back, saying, "No sir, tis not good fur; my dogs wouldn't run such a coon, nor bark at a man that was fool enough to carry such a skin." Crockett continued to stress that he had been a good steward, looking out for the people of West Tennessee. He was the same man they had elected in the past, but more experienced. There could be no disguising his abandonment of Andrew Jackson and the Democrats, however, and this cost him dearly.

On election day, Crockett went to McLemoresville to cast his ballot amidst rumors that the Democrats were paying twenty-five dollars a vote. The results were not known until August 9. Crockett had 4,400 votes, but Adam Huntsman had 4,652. Not only had he lost the election for Congress, but his chances of running for president also were ruined. Feeling sorry for himself, he exclaimed, "I have no doubt that I was completely raskaled out of my election." When asked what he would do next, he responded, "The rest of you can go to Hell, for I am going to Texas." In September, he told the press, "I never expect to offer my name again to the public for any office."

Having made the remark about Texas, his present circumstances began to bear down on him. He had been a national figure for ten years, and the prospects of being an impoverished farmer were unappealing. He could go on a trip to Texas and scout the land and hunt the game there. Perhaps he could hunt buffalo, long since disappeared from West Tennessee. And he could mix with old friends like Sam Houston. Nothing said he had to stay in Texas, but to go there would be a real adventure. Surely he was aware of the growing fight for Texas independence, but that was their fight, not his, and he must have realized that Texas would one day be a state and that he might revive his political fortunes there.

Prior to leaving, Crockett gave himself a send-off party at his Gibson County farm with a large barbecue. While cooks tended the cooking of the meat, the guests dipped gourds in a barrel of whiskey and competed in logrolling contests. Crockett played the fiddle, told stories, and repeated what was now becoming a theme for him: He had done his best to get elected, but had been rejected. Accordingly, the voters could go to Hell; he was going to Texas.

By October 31, he was ready to leave. He was joined by a nephew, William Patton, and two neighbors. Bidding farewell to his family, he said he would send for them if he liked what he saw in Texas. He made no mention of the uprising there against the Mexican government. Clad in his hunting suit and mounted on a large chestnut horse with a white star on his forehead, he rode away on the first day of November.

Traveling south, the group rode through Jackson and on to Bolivar, where they spent the night. As they journeyed on, the night sky put on a show of its own as Halley's Comet passed overhead. Turning west, they reached Memphis on November 10. Finding old friends and acquaintances there, they began to tour the city, going from bar to bar. When the party reached Neil McCool's saloon, they carried Crockett in on their shoulders and deposited him on the bar, where he gave a speech. Repeating the "go to hell, I am going to Texas" refrain, he ended by saying, "I am on my way now."

The next morning, with aching heads, they crossed the Mississippi River by ferry to the Arkansas shore. On a well-traveled road, they covered the 120 miles to Little Rock in two days.

In Little Rock, Crockett was treated as a celebrity. The townspeople hosted his party to a dinner, with speeches after the meal. Among Whigs and anti-Jackson people, Crockett felt at home and lambasted the Democrats. He talked at length about his recent defeat and had little to say about the revolution in Texas. One reporter swore, however, that Crockett boasted he would "have Santa Anna's head and use it for a watch seal." Going southwest the next day, he headed toward the Red River, where he crossed to the Mexican side at a place called Lost Prairie. (Remember that what is now Texas, where Crockett crossed, was Mexican territory at the time and the settlers called themselves Texans.)

By early December, he had passed through Clarksville, Texas, and decided to set off across country to hunt. It would be his first chance to hunt bison and Texas bears. There were no white settlements in the region, only Kickapoo Indians. Riding eighty miles west, he found the land so pleasing that he began to talk about never returning to Tennessee. The bison migrated through the land twice a year, and there were swarms of wild bees that produced enough honey for a man and also served as a lure for bears. Before setting off, he agreed to rendezvous with the others of his party by Christmas at the falls of the Brazos. When he failed to show up, rumors began to spread that he had been killed by the Kickapoos. By February, reports of his death reached the eastern press. Contrary to the rumors, he was enjoying his hunt so much that he ignored the deadline for the rendezvous.

By January 5, Crockett was in Nacogdoches, where the townsmen welcomed him, assuming he had come to join the revolution. It was a happy time in his life for a number of reasons. He was in the best of health. After seeing the Choctaw

Bayou–Bois D'Arc Creek (where he had been on his hunting trip), he liked the land so much that he began thinking he might be appointed as a land agent and have his friends settle there around him. Also, he was free from the burden of being anti-Jackson. American politics stopped at the Sabine River, and Texans cared only about what was happening in Texas. (Early skirmishes had pushed the Mexican Army back across the Rio Grande, though Santa Anna was rumored to be on the way with another army.)

After a few days in Nacogdoches, Crockett and about ten followers rode east to San Augustine, where another welcoming dinner awaited him. The civic leaders suggested that he become a candidate to represent them in the March 1 constitutional convention. From this, Crockett realized that he could play a major role in Texas politics, if he so desired.

Now, too, the lure of adventure began to tug at him. He assumed that he would receive a generous land bounty if he chose to join the volunteer military forces. He was forty-nine years old, and it had been twenty years since his last military campaign. He would enjoy the excitement of a fight or two—it would be a last chance to return to the days of his youth. He could do a little fighting, electioneer at the same time, and win a seat in the coming convention. It would be the start of his new political career.

On January 4, Crockett and his friends returned to Nacogdoches and took the oath of allegiance to the provisional government of Texas. In so doing, he committed his future to Texas. After this, he told people he never intended to return to Tennessee again. At a dinner, he told the ladies of the town that the Texas men would "lick up the Mexicans like fine salt" and he personally would "grin all of the Mexicans out of Texas."

After his enlistment, a band of other volunteers from Tennessee surrounded him, calling themselves the Tennessee Mounted Volunteers. By January 16, they had their equipment and were ready to go. In a letter back to Tennessee, David wrote, "I am rejoiced at my fate. Do not be uneasy about me, I am with my friends."

Thus, David Crockett rode away toward the revolution and to the Alamo. By the morning of March 6, it was all over, and Crockett and all of the Tennesseans were dead. If he had not been killed at the Alamo, perhaps he would have started a new political career and become a wealthy man with large land grants. Certainly, he would have been a powerful figure in the new Republic after Texas gained its independence from Mexico. Would he have ever returned to Tennessee? Perhaps not!

Crockett was quite a character—a true hero of the frontier. And though his life ended before he turned fifty, his death at the Alamo only added to the legend and made his life seem even bigger.

Modern Bridge on Natchez Trace Parkway near Franklin, Tennessee

The Great Road

Much of our history is found
along the old river channels and land trails. Starting as little
more than animal paths, then traveled by Indians and early
settlers, they became our pathways of history. Though we have
many trails, the most prominent is the Natchez Trace.

In 1799, Winthrop Sargent, the first governor of the
Mississippi Territory, suggested that a post road from Natchez,
Mississippi, to Knoxville, Tennessee, be built to improve
communications with the nation's capital. The original road ran
from the port of Natchez on the Mississippi River along 500
miles of Indian paths, through
the Choctaw and Chickasaw
nations, across the Tennessee
River to Nashville.

Congress readily agreed that the road was needed, but delayed construction until they could gain permission to cross Indian land. The Chickasaws and Choctaws gave permission, but the Cherokees refused to let the road cross their lands from Nashville to Knoxville. Nashville thus became the northern end of the road. From Natchez, the Trace ran northward to Bayou Pierre, east of Vicksburg. It then turned toward the northeast for 160 miles through the Choctaw Nation and then ran for 205 miles through the Chickasaw Nation. The final segment ran along a thinly settled trail in Tennessee. Despite improvements on both ends, much of the Trace remained as little more than a horse trail. Under the leadership of General James Wilkinson, Edmund Pendleton Gaines marked the path through the Indian lands in 1802. Army troops were used to widen the trail.

Though originally designed as a means to improve communications to Washington, the nature of the road soon changed. When flatboats floated down the Mississippi, their crews had to get back upstream by land through Mississippi and Alabama to Nashville. With their pockets full of gold coins from the sale of their boats and goods, they were easy prey for bands of robbers and thieves.

The Tennessee militia used the Trace at least three times. In 1803, troops marched to Natchez as a precaution when the Louisiana Purchase occurred. In 1813, John Coffee led his cavalry along the Trace to join Andrew Jackson during the War of 1812. When ordered to dismiss his troops, Jackson defiantly marched them up the Trace, earning him the nickname of "Old Hickory" because he was tougher than a hickory nut. In 1815, following the Battle of New Orleans, Jackson again led his Tennessee troops up the Trace.

Far more than a road from Natchez to Nashville, the Trace had a major effect on many distant cities and territories. It served as a route for supplies for Pittsburgh, St. Louis, and cities in Oklahoma, where the Chickasaws and Choctaws were pushed. Men going west to die at the Alamo never dreamed what lay before them. In addition to the Army, the Postmaster General contracted with businessmen to deliver the mail from Nashville to Natchez. The businessmen would then contract with hired riders who made the trip in ten to fifteen days' time.

More than anything, the Trace was home for the happy-go-lucky boatmen returning home after drunken celebrations in Natchez and New Orleans. The most colorful of the boatmen was a character named Mike Fink. Mark Twain described him as being half alligator and half horse! No portrait is available of him, but it seems unlikely that any man could have beaten him in a fight, gouged out one of his eyes, or bitten off one of his ears. Mark Twain in *Life on the Mississippi* recorded a typical battle cry:

"Look at Me! I'm the man they call Sudden Death and General Desolation! Sired by a hurricane, dam'd by an earthquake, half-brother to the cholera, nearly related to the smallpox on the mother's side! Look at me! I take nineteen alligators and a bar'l of whiskey

for breakfast when I'm in robust health, and a bushel of rattlesnakes and a dead body when I'm ailing. I split the everlasting rocks with my glance, and I quench the thunder when I speak! Whoo-oop! Stand back and give me room according to my strength! Blood's my natural drink, and the wails of the dying is music to my ear. Cast your eye on me, gentlemen! And lay low and hold your breath, for I'm about to turn myself loose!"

By the late 1820s, the Trace was no longer heavily traveled, though local traffic used segments of it for decades. Reasons for its demise were changing settlement locations, competing roads, and steamboat travel. In May of 1938, the Natchez Trace Parkway, a unit of the National Park Service, was established to commemorate the historical significance of the Trace. Just over 100 miles of the old road is located in Tennessee, running through Davidson, Williamson, Hickman, Maury, Lewis, and Wayne counties.

The Choctaws and Chickasaws are long gone, as are the soldiers, river boatmen, robbers, and gamblers. Yet for twenty-five years, they were a part of one of the most colorful periods of our heritage.

Skulls of Samuel Mason and Wiley Harpe on the Natchez Trace

Death on the Trace

For a quarter of a century, the Natchez Trace was one of the most traveled roads in America. From 1803 through the late 1820s, pioneers, politicians, prostitutes, robbers, and soldiers marched along it. Given the colorful nature of the characters, life was cheap and murder sometimes seemed too easy. Gold-laden boatmen coming home from Natchez and New Orleans were easy prey for robbers and cheats and helped the Trace to acquire a dark and bloody reputation.

The Harpe brothers were two of the most notorious outlaws in Tennessee history. Born in North Carolina, they came west to Kentucky and East Tennessee in 1795. They were dark-skinned with curly hair, which some felt gave them the appearance of having African bloodlines. Micajah was the older of the two, with the nickname of "Big Harpe." The younger brother was named Wiley and was called "Little Harpe." Not only did they rob and murder people, they tortured and mutilated their victims. Their specialty was opening the bodies of their victims, filling them with rocks, and sinking them in swamps or rivers. Even their fellow desperadoes disapproved of the savagery of their crimes and tried to catch them. Once as a joke, they tied a victim to his horse and chased the animal over a cliff. Shortly after this, Big Harpe tomahawked a fellow lodger because he snored too loudly and then, for good measure, killed the woman of the tavern with her baby. A furious posse caught them just as they were robbing yet another victim. Little Harpe managed to escape, but a bullet in the spine paralyzed Big Harpe. The husband of the victim then began to cut Big Harpe's head off with a butcher knife. Big Harpe is said to have responded, "You're a damned rough butcher, but cut on an' be damned." Harpe's head was nailed to a fork in a tree near Henderson, Kentucky, where it grinned at travelers for years.

Wiley Harpe continued his career of robbing and killing travelers along the Trace after joining up with another killer, Samuel Mason. Mason had turned criminal late in life, having been a respectable citizen and justice of the peace as well as a soldier who fought against both the British and the Indians.

In 1803, Mason was captured but escaped during a storm while being transported to Natchez. Shortly thereafter, two men

Meriwether Lewis

brought in a lump of blue clay containing the head of Samuel Mason, requesting a $2,000 reward that had been placed on him. John Bowman of Tennessee recognized Little Harpe as one of the men, and, after a pursuit, Harpe was captured. Harpe, along with his partner, was hung in Gallows Field in Greenville. The heads of the two killers were placed on stakes on the Trace near Greenville, Mississippi.

With the Harpe brothers now reduced to grinning skulls, the number of murders and robberies slowed down. Even so, most people still traveled in convoys.

In 1809, the most unusual death on the Trace occurred when Meriwether Lewis died. Lewis was only thirty-five years old, and his death was both untimely and mysterious. Just five years earlier, he had been the co-leader of the Voyage of Discovery with William Clark. Known as the Lewis and Clark Expedition, they were the first white men to explore the country's most northwest wilderness after the United States bought the Louisiana Territory from France in 1803. The trip lasted more than two years and covered 7,700 miles! In 1807, Thomas Jefferson appointed Lewis governor of the Louisiana Territory.

Lewis left St. Louis with two servants in September of 1809, intending to travel to Washington to answer complaints about his action as governor. On October 8, they crossed the Tennessee River and began traveling on the Trace. Reaching Grinders Tavern on the evening of October 11, they were seventy-three miles south of Nashville in Tennessee, just inside United States territory beyond the Chickasaw land.

During the night, two shots were heard from the room where Lewis was sleeping. He died early the next morning from a gunshot to the head. Though the tragedy was reported to Thomas Jefferson as a suicide, others felt that an assassin had shot him. Another report stated that in addition to the gunshot, his throat had been cut.

The death of Lewis by suicide was not publicly challenged until 1848, when Tennessee moved the site of his grave and constructed a monument over it. This monument is now a part of the Natchez Trace Parkway. Even today, the debate continues over whether he committed suicide or was murdered. In 1996, a group of forensic scientists convinced a Lewis County coroner's jury to request approval of his descendants for the body to be exhumed to determine the cause of his death. Family dissension prevented this from happening. We may never know what happened that night. Still, it seems ironic that Meriwether Lewis, called by many as the greatest pathfinder this country has ever known, should die on a lonely road in Tennessee.

Confederate Powder Magazine at Randolph

They Could Have Been Memphis

Have you ever been to Randolph? I doubt it. Have you ever heard of Randolph? Probably not. In fact, very few people who live in West Tennessee know about Randolph, and yet, Randolph once had the opportunity to become the largest city in Tennessee! What became of that opportunity is a sad story.

In the early to mid-1800s, there were two Tennessee towns that were competing for supremacy on the Mississippi River. These towns were Memphis and Randolph. Memphis is situated on the fourth Chickasaw Bluff while Randolph is sixty miles up river on the second Chickasaw Bluff. Memphis is located in Shelby County; Randolph is in Tipton County.

Randolph is named for John Randolph of Virginia. It was first settled in 1823, when Jesse Benton established a trading post there almost thirty years after the settlement of Memphis. It is located four miles south of the mouth of the Hatchie River, known locally as the "Big Hatchie." Traders from all over West Tennessee floated down the Hatchie bringing their furs and hides to the Benton trading post at Randolph.

The town was incorporated in 1831. By 1835, they had a newspaper, *The Randolph Recorder,* the first in the county. Early town laws included a tax of three dollars for every male between the ages of eighteen and forty-five, two dollars per day to store boats at the landing, and a fine of five dollars to twenty-five dollars for gambling with cards. By 1830, three warehouses, six dry good stores, ten doctors, a tavern, and twenty to thirty families were located there. (You would have to wonder why so many doctors lived there!) By 1834, four hotels were in business. By 1835, the population had grown to 1,000, and by 1840, there were several private schools, one being called a college.

Randolph had an ideal landing site on the Mississippi River. Additionally, its close proximity to the Hatchie, one of the most navigable rivers in West Tennessee, where steamboats could go as far as sixty miles up river to Bolivar, began to attract a large amount of commerce. The main commodity that passed through Randolph was cotton. Until 1836, Randolph not only shipped more cotton than Memphis, but also served as the steamboat depot of West Tennessee. As an example, the December 19, 1834, issue of *The Randolph Recorder* reported a record of 3,504 bales shipped the previous week, along with forty tons of iron valued at $220,000.

Randolph seemed to have many advantages over Memphis. Randolph was blessed with trade from the Hatchie, while

Memphis had the Wolf River, much shorter than the Hatchie. Randolph had a better landing site, which traders and flatboat operators preferred, and Randolph seemed to be immune to yellow fever and other diseases that swept through Memphis. The very atmosphere in Randolph seemed to be more soft and graceful, while Memphis had all of the characteristics of a tough, brawling river town. It was obvious that Randolph had a wonderful future. It seemed destined to become a great city. And then, it all slipped away. In less than twenty years, Randolph would go from one of Tennessee's largest commercial centers to little more than a ghost town. How could that happen?

Five years after its founding, the land title to Randolph was discovered to be faulty. A Mrs. Grambrelling of New York filed suit to claim the whole town on the grounds she had acquired a military land grant warrant to the tract. Her case stood up in court. The original owner of the land grant was a Negro Revolutionary War veteran, which added to the unusual nature of the suit. The litigation lasted for more than a year. In a compromise settlement, a group of Randolph citizens bought their town back for $8,000. Even though the suit was settled, it slowed progress.

Another thing went wrong when Covington was selected as the county seat because of Covington's central location in the county, whereas Randolph was on the edge of the county. In 1835, Lauderdale County was formed, and the northern part of Tipton County became part of Lauderdale, leaving Covington no longer in the middle of the county. Citizens from Randolph petitioned the General Assembly to change the county seat from Covington to Randolph. Accordingly, an election was held in 1852. When the votes were counted, Covington was the winner. In 1854, citizens from Randolph petitioned for another election, and Covington won again. The county seat would remain in Covington.

In 1826, before Randolph was founded, Congress approved a military road from Memphis to Little Rock. The project took so long to materialize that Randolph could have captured the position as starting point from Memphis anytime up to 1835. Randolph failed to do so. As overland travel to Texas increased, Memphis continued to grow.

The Post Office Department in Washington established a tri-weekly mail route to Memphis by way of Jackson, Bolivar, Somerville, and Raleigh. Another route was set up from Jackson to Memphis through Brownsville, Covington, and Randolph, but this route was traveled only once a week. At the time, both routes were thinly settled, but people migrated toward the postal road that was serviced three times a week. As a result, the growth and trade of Memphis increased while Randolph remained stationary.

Between the years of 1834 and 1838, three events spelled Randolph's doom. In the Treaty of 1834, the Chickasaw Indians were forced to leave their homes in North Mississippi. The removal of the Chickasaws opened the land up for growing cotton and for the expansion of the railroads. The rapid settlement of the area increased the business and population of Memphis while Randolph continued as a shipping point for a much smaller area.

In 1835, Governor Newton Cannon proposed a canal project that would connect the Hatchie River to the Tennessee River. The canal was to start two miles above Hamburg on the Tennessee River and strike the Hatchie where it joined Tuscumbia Creek. The project would have carried all of the trade from North Alabama and the Tennessee Valley to the Mississippi River at Randolph. Though the legislature appropriated $1,500 for a survey, the canal was never built due to a prevailing sentiment from Washington that no federal monies be appropriated for internal improvement projects.

In 1833, railroad promoters proposed the building of a line from the interior of West Tennessee to a port on the Mississippi River, primarily to transport cotton. Politics prevailed, and the line went to Memphis. Though the line eventually failed, the image of Randolph as a trade center was tarnished. It would be 1859 before a rail line crossed any part of Tipton County. Randolph never got rail service.

The crash of 1837 was a financial collapse that affected all of the country, but it seemed to hit Randolph much harder than Memphis. At the time it occurred, Randolph still had twenty-two businesses and was the business center for that part of the country. As the businesses declined, the trade seemed to shift to Memphis.

The final catastrophic event of the 1830s was the changing of the river channel. The channel had been slowly moving away from the bluff, and by 1838, the harbor was so far out that cotton shipping and steamboat trade generally was diverted to Memphis. This diversion of cotton to Memphis hurt Randolph economically. If there was no cotton to ship, no money was made, and if no money was pumped into the economy, the town suffered.

In an incident that occurred in 1845 at the Planters Hotel in Randolph, a stranger imparted some of his thoughts to the local residents. The stranger said, "I have traveled much, I have crossed the Atlantic six times, I have been to Europe, Asia, Africa, and America and have observed one thing about your town." The locals asked, "What?" The stranger replied, "It is finished." The stranger was right.

In April of 1861, Governor Isham G. Harris ordered Lieutenant Colonel Marcus Wright, 154th Militia Regiment (Confederate) at Memphis, to proceed north and occupy a defensive position on the Mississippi River with a battalion of infantry and supporting artillery. Over the next four months, some 4,000 troops from Arkansas and Tennessee fortified the bluff with entrenchments and artillery positions against an expected Union naval and land attack. For these four months, Fort Wright was the forward-most Confederate position on the Mississippi River, serving as a training camp for new recruits. Two soldiers who would one day be Confederate lieutenant generals were there briefly, those being Alexander P. Stewart and Nathan Bedford Forest. Though named Fort Wright, the soldiers called it Camp Yellowjacket because of the number of vicious insects along the bluff. By 1862, the fort was abandoned, though Confederate cavalry and naval forces continued to occupy it on an irregular basis.

In September of 1862, a small group of ten to fifteen Confederates fired at a Union ship, the packet *Eugene,* when it landed at Randolph. No damage was done, but the act so enraged General William T. Sherman, commander for the district with headquarters at Memphis, that he issued orders for Randolph to be burned. On September 24, Colonel Charles Walcott and the 46th Ohio burned every home in Randolph except one home belonging to J. H. Barton. Each resident was allowed a small amount of time to remove belongings. In one case, an elderly woman who was sick was carried out in her bed! When the Ohio soldiers left, some twenty families were left homeless on the bluff. Legend has it that the one house left standing belonged to a Mason who was a member of the same lodge as Colonel Walcott. The next day, Sherman reported, "The regiment has returned and Randolph is gone."

Two years later, a group of forty Confederates attempted to capture the steamer *Belle Saint Louis* when it landed at Randolph. On board were six Federal paymasters with $40,000 in currency, which the Confederates desperately needed. The attempt failed. It was the last action of the Civil War to occur in Randolph. Ironically, for Tipton County, the war had begun and ended at Randolph.

After the war, Randolph tried to pick itself up and start over. In 1874, the town had a population of 300, along with a post office, stores, schools, and churches. It was still an important point for receiving and shipping merchandise and produce. The town was destroyed by fire again in 1885. The town was reincorporated on March 19, 1913. Its tenure was short-lived, for on February 2, 1921, the town's charter was abolished.

This past May, I went to Randolph. If you are going to be there at lunchtime, you had better take it with you. I did, having stopped at a country store in Burlison for a bologna and "rat cheese" sandwich. The river is the main attraction because there's not much else there—a half dozen houses, two historical markers, and a church. On that day, the Mississippi was at flood stage and had an angry look to it. Up on the bluff, deep in a thicket, we found the old powder magazine, all that remains of Fort Wright. For all practical purposes, Randolph is gone—a town (almost a city) that existed long ago. But if you stay a while upon the bluff, the past seems to whisper to you of hopes and dreams of another time.

An Empty Coffin

A Most Unusual Funeral

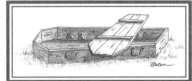

Through the years, I have written a lot of stories about the little town of Denmark. Located about twenty minutes southwest of the Jackson airport, it is one of my favorite places. Once, Denmark rivaled Jackson in size and prosperity. Through the years, Denmark has shrunk. Today, fewer than a dozen people live there. All that remains is the Presbyterian Church, the post office, and two residences. For years, Robert Hardee had a grocery store that shared a frame building with the post office, where his wife was postmistress. When Robert died, the building was abandoned. His wife, Alta Ruth, continued her duties in a new post office building next door until her death.

Not long ago, on a Saturday night, a driver missed a stop sign and plowed into the old store and post office, demolishing it. I had eaten a lot of sandwiches in that store through the years. I will miss it.

Next door to the old store is the residence of the Hardees. The house was built in 1846 by Dan Harbert, one of two brothers who owned and operated one of the largest grocery and hardware stores in the Big Hatchie Country. John Harbert was Dan's older brother and partner. John's son, Billy, was employed in the store as a clerk.

Merchandise for the store came from places as far away as Cincinnati and Louisville. To obtain the merchandise, it was necessary to go to the city to purchase it. Accordingly, young Billy Harbert was sent to Cincinnati with enough currency to buy what was needed.

To reach Cincinnati required travel by steamboat. While on the boat, Billy began to gamble and lost all of the money in a crooked card game. Feeling guilty and unable to face his father and uncle, Billy persuaded the captain of the boat to send a letter back to Denmark stating that he had fallen overboard and drowned.

The period of mourning for Billy was barely over before Billy showed up at the store very humble, confessing his guilt and begging forgiveness. His uncle, Dan, agreed to forgive him if he would make a public apology. The old Billy Harbert, with his faults and guilt, was to be buried.

On the day of the funeral, an empty casket was carried by six slaves from Dan Harbert's house across the street to the Presbyterian Church, where it was placed before the altar.

Reverend Gillespie prayed: "Dust to dust, ashes to ashes, and may the sins and faults of Billy Harbert never arise again." The empty casket was then carried to the Baptist cemetery and buried.

This version of Billy Harbert's funeral comes from a newspaper article written years ago by Fonville Neville, a longtime resident of Denmark. Another version of the story was more dramatic. In that version, news of Billy's gambling loss preceded his return to Denmark. When he got home, to his distress, a funeral procession was crossing the front yard of his home. When he asked who had died, he was told that it was the "old" Billy Harbert. You can imagine his shock.

Billy Harbert got a second chance and was a credit to the town and his family for the remainder of his life. Have you ever wished you could bury your old self and start over?

Thomas Alva Edison

Thomas Alva Edison in Tennessee

For years, local historians have argued about the possibility that Thomas Alva Edison once lived in Jackson. The story goes that he worked here as a telegraph operator for the railroad, moving from Jackson to Bolivar and from there to Grand Junction. Jim Driver, a Jackson railroad historian, tells of a conversation with Coley Chandler, an engineer with the Illinois Central Railroad, who remembered Edison's living here. He pointed to a vacant lot on Baltimore Street as the site where Edison lived in a boarding house. Could the "Wizard of Menlo Park" have lived here? Edison has been described as the greatest inventor in history. Is it possible he once lived in Jackson, if only for a brief period?

During his lifetime, Edison patented 1,093 inventions! He had only three months of formal schooling, but his inventions of the phonograph and electric light changed the lives of millions of people. Henry Ford suggested that the period of Edison's life should be known as the "Age of Edison." Edison downplayed this, saying that genius was "one percent inspiration and ninety-nine percent perspiration." He demonstrated this by working for days at a time, stopping only for short naps. He seemed to be interested in everything around him, even experimenting in the field of medicine. He came close to the invention of the radio and predicted the use of atomic energy. Besides his own inventions, he improved the inventions of others, including the telephone, the typewriter, the motion picture, the electric generator, and the electric-powered train.

Edison was born in Milan, Ohio, in 1847, the youngest of seven children. Born with an intense curiosity about everything, he irritated his public school teacher by asking endless questions. When the schoolmaster described him as being "addled," his mother took him out of school and taught him at home. When his mother could not answer his questions, he would try to answer them with experiments. One day, after learning that balloons fly because they are filled with gas, he persuaded a friend to take a triple dose of laxative powder to see if he would fly. Obviously, he did not, becoming ill instead!

By the time he was twelve, he was selling newspapers and food on the Grand Trunk Railway between Port Huron and Detroit. One day, he set a baggage car on fire while experimenting with phosphorus sticks. The conductor boxed his ears and threw him off the train. The conductor's blows may have lead to his loss of hearing, a condition that grew worse as he grew older. Being unable to hear did not bother him, as it made it easier for him to concentrate.

After losing his job on the railroad, Edison sold newspapers at stations along the Grand Trunk Railway. One day at the Mt. Clemons, Michigan, station, Edison rescued the stationmaster's son from being run over by a freight car. The grateful stationmaster taught Edison how to tap out messages on a telegraph key. Learning to be a telegraph operator led to a new career. It probably led him to Tennessee!

Edison's first telegraph assignment was on the Grand Trunk Railway in Toronto, Canada, when he was only sixteen. In the fall of 1863, he returned to the United States. During the years from 1863 to 1866, Edison, like many young men, drifted from city to city as an itinerant, or "tramp," telegrapher. Throughout the country, there was a need for telegraphers because so many experienced operators were serving in the Civil War.

Given what we know of the short time Edison spent in the South, when could he have been in West Tennessee?

The most logical scenario would have been for Edison to have come south to West Tennessee from Cincinnati, then move up the tracks from Jackson to Bolivar to Grand Junction and then on to Memphis. This would have placed him here in the latter part of 1865.

In an article in *The Bolivar Bulletin Times*, written in February 1980 by County Historian Faye Davidson, she clearly states that Edison spent time in Bolivar:

"Until he was twenty he was a 'hoboing telegrapher.' He liked to take the night shift as this afforded less interruption to study and carry out his experimental theories. During these roving years Edison came to Bolivar and secured a job as a telegrapher at the depot. Immediately he set up a laboratory in the rooms, which he used as his sleeping quarters. This was not unusual for the young man to request. One quiet, peaceful night a terrible explosion rocked the vicinity. People awakened to find the whole end of the depot blown off from Edison's 'tomfoolery'! Needless to say, a telegrapher was once again on his way to a new experimental site."

Paul Israel is the managing editor of the multi-volume documentary edition of the *Thomas Edison Papers* at Rutgers University and the author of two books on Edison. When I e-mailed him about Edison in West Tennessee, he responded, "I have never seen any reference to Edison being anywhere in Tennessee other than Memphis. It is certainly possible, given the chaotic situation in Tennessee at that time, that he might have briefly worked as a railway telegrapher in Bolivar. But it seems more likely that he was just passing through." In a later e-mail, he wrote, "Edison was in his early 60s when he wrote his reminiscences. It is entirely possible he briefly stayed in these towns before settling for a while in Memphis. Though, of course, it is debatable whether one can say he was living rather than visiting there."

I believe that Thomas Edison lived and worked as a telegraph operator in West Tennessee for a short period just after the end of the Civil War in 1865. I hoped to find some definitive bit of evidence, but the trail was too cold and too many years had passed by. However, if he was not here, why all of these old stories about his presence in Jackson and Bolivar?

In the 1970s, Jackson telephone books carried a brief history of the city. In that history was a statement that Edison had spent time here as a telegraph operator. Surely, if "Ma Bell" says it, then it must be true!

Edison's tracks in Memphis are much easier to follow. In September of 1865, Edison was a press operator with the Cincinnati Branch of the National Telegraphic Union. From there, a streak of wanderlust led him south into the chaos of the end of the Civil War. In his memoirs, written more than forty years later, he claimed that he headed directly for Memphis. Other evidence suggests that he spent the last three months of 1865 in Nashville. At any rate, Edison was in Memphis through the first months of 1866.

The 1866 *Memphis City Directory* shows Edison as a resident of the city, listing him as "Edison, T. A., telegraph operator, 40 N. Court." Other evidence to support this is found in the flyleaves of books he purchased there in March of that year.

Judge J. P. Young, a Memphis historian, remembered Edison as "walking with his head always bent forward at a sharp angle, having very little to say to anyone, wearing an old slouch hat, a linen duster usually spattered with ink that reached to his ankles, and almost shapeless shoes.

Edison always attracted attention as he walked about the streets of Memphis in those days but in the way that a 'town character' usually does. Edison was looked upon by his fellow townsmen as a sort of 'bug' or crank. People were inclined to laugh when his name was mentioned, both because of his peculiar appearance and because it was known that he spent most of his spare time working on some inventions. If we had been asked to select one man in town destined to become a figure of international importance, Edison probably would have been the last one any of us would have thought of. Thomas Edison was a sight. He had the most peculiar appearance you ever saw. With his queer clothes and thoughtful mien, he would sit for hours just thinking."

Life in Memphis was chaotic at best as it moved from military to civilian government. Racial strife, lawlessness, and violence prevailed, and he described the town as being "only 13 miles from Hell!" Years later, Edison remembered Memphis as follows: "Everything (in Memphis) at that time was wide open. Disorganization reigned supreme. There was no head to anything. At night, a companion and myself would go over to a gorgeously furnished faro bank (gambling establishment) and get our midnight lunch. Everything (the food) was free. There were 20 keno rooms running and one of them that I visited was in a Baptist church, the man with the wheel being in the pulpit and the gamblers in the pews. About 30,000 Negroes slept on the levee every night, and everything was 'red hot.'"

Though Edison was shy and awkward, he was a wizard as a telegraph operator whose speed at sending and receiving messages far exceeded any of the veteran operators. Edison worked as a night telegraph operator in the United States Military Telegraph Service. The office was in a newspaper building at 40 North Court Street, and he boarded next door.

Edison's distaste for doing dull or repetitive tasks led to his first real invention. In the Memphis office, one telegraph circuit ran to New York, while another ran to New Orleans. Because of the distance, a message could not be sent directly from New York to New Orleans. It annoyed Edison that it was necessary to copy messages never intended for Memphis, acting as a relay between the two cities. Working with bits of wire and batteries, he invented an automatic relay. The device should have been worth thousands of dollars, but he was unaware of patents or of the value of his invention. (He was making only seventy-five dollars a month at the time.)

Another invention perfected during his Memphis stay was a trap to electrocute cockroaches by stringing wires across the office and charging them with electricity.

In April of 1866, Edison moved to Louisville, ending his stay in Tennessee. Barely in his twenties and still dressed in a linen duster and battered straw hat, the greatest inventor in history was just beginning his glorious career. Few people remember Edison's days in Tennessee, yet for a short time, the "Wizard of Menlo Park" was part of our history!

One Sabbath morning during the civil war two young soldiers of the Seventh Tennessee Cavalry occupied this pew with their sweethearts. When the federal soldiers surrounded the church and searched the building, the two soldiers escaped capture by hiding under the hoopskirts of the young ladies.

Denmark Presbyterian Church

The Valentine Story

When I think of Valentine's Day and romance, my thoughts turn to the old Presbyterian Church in Denmark. In the midst of the Civil War, two young soldiers, members of the 7th Tennessee Cavalry, returned home to visit their sweethearts. As they accompanied the girls to church, any thoughts of love or religion soon disappeared when they found the church surrounded by Yankee soldiers. There was but one place to hide, and under the girls' hoop skirts they went. They were not discovered and soon returned to their regiment, but can you not imagine the stories they told of their hiding place?

Today, you can visit the church and see where this happened. Go down the right aisle and look on the left side, three pews from the front. A bronze marker commemorates the spot of romance and terror of long ago.

Confederate Veterans Monument in Jackson, Tennessee

ERECTED 1888

TO THE
CONFEDERATE
DEAD
OF
MADISON COUNTY

R Brown

The Sixth Tennessee Infantry, CSA
The West Tennessee Regiment

During the four years of the Civil War, eighty Tennessee infantry Confederate units were formed. Of this number, seventeen regiments were comprised primarily of West Tennessee soldiers. Five of these regiments, the 6th, 9th, 12th, 13th, and 15th, were activated and trained at Camp Beauregard in Jackson. (Look for the historical marker at the corner of Airways and Hollywood.) Of these regiments, I think of the 6th Tennessee as being "West Tennessee's regiment" because of their record during the war and their hometowns.

The regiment was organized on May 23, 1861, and was the first unit to occupy Camp Beauregard. It was composed of eleven companies, one from Somerville, one from Brownsville, one from Gadsden, and the rest from Madison County. The colorful names of the companies reflect the patriotism and excitement of the early months of the war. Company A from Fayette County called themselves the Somerville Avengers. Company C chose the name of Madison Invincibles. While men from Crockett County were named the Gadsden Spartans, Company K from Denmark, in Madison County, called themselves the Danes.

One by one, the companies said their "good-byes" in their communities and either marched into Jackson or were brought in by wagons.

John Johnston, a recruit in the Denmark Danes, had this remembrance of going off to war:

"Some weeks were spent in drilling and dress parades and undergoing the plaudits and admiration of our friends and sweethearts. Until about the first of May, when we received orders to go into Camp at Jackson. Up to this time we had had a gala time but things now began to grow serious. We must now leave home and go—we knew not where not to what fate. A day was appointed for our departure. It was a lovely spring day. The whole community—men, women and children were assembled at the church that day.

The minister took his text from 1st Kings XXII: 34—

'And a certain man drew a bow at a venture and smote the King of Israel between the joints of the harness'— and preached therefrom what to me was a very tender and comforting sermon.

The services being over, we were marched out and drawn up in line in front of the gate of the church yard and facing the church where Miss Emma Cobb presented the Company with a beautiful silk flag with the name of the Company painted on it—accompanying the presentation with a little speech prepared for the occasion. Capt. Ingram received the flag and responded with a brief speech.

This over we proceeded to tell our friends and loved ones goodbye. And now came to me a great surprise—our mothers and sisters, who up to this time had stood quietly by, now began to weep in the most mournful manner.

These sad farewells having been said, we climbed into the farm wagons that had been prepared to transport us to Jackson—and drove away with the lamentations of our loved ones sounding in our ears."

William H. Stephens was elected colonel of the regiment. An attorney from Jackson, he was clerk of the Supreme Court of Tennessee from 1840 to 1857. Active in politics, during the campaign of 1856, Stephens was involved in opposing James Buchanan, the Democratic candidate for President. In addition to law and politics, Stephens served as a director and president of the Union Bank at Jackson. His brother and a son also served in the regiment with him.

The regiment was present at the Battle of Belmont, Kentucky, in November but did not take part. Following the evacuation of Columbus, Kentucky, the regiment moved to Corinth, Mississippi. On April 6, the regiment got its wish, at last, to go up against the enemy. Can you not imagine their excitement as they marched to Shiloh, where General Grant and the Army of the Tennessee was camped at Pittsburg Landing? Marching all day on the fifth, the men did not come into the Confederate lines until late at night. The following morning, the regiment was in line of battle from daylight to ten o'clock, moving from the center to the left wing several times. While waiting in reserve, the unit was subjected to heavy artillery fire. Here, they suffered their first casualties. The first to be wounded was J. M. Cartmell, who was struck in the face by a shell fragment that destroyed his left eye. (Cartmell was the brother of Robert Cartmell, Jackson's diarist who kept a diary of life in Jackson for sixty-five years.) Cartmell recovered from his wound, though blind in one eye, and lived in Jackson until 1913, when he was hit and killed by a car!

About eleven o'clock, orders were received to charge an artillery battery in their front. Concealed in the woods in front of them, in what would come to be known as the Sunken Road, was the 14th Iowa under the command of William T. Shaw, a Mexican War veteran. When the unit was within thirty paces of the woods, the Iowa soldiers fired a volley into them. The result was terrible. In seconds, 250 men lay dead in the line of battle, as if they were on dress parade, sadly recalled one of the survivors. Colonel Stephens had his horse shot from under him, and his son, William, who was on his staff, was severely wounded. The color-bearer was killed, and all twelve members of the color guard were killed or wounded. The flag was shot to shreds, and the staff that held it was hit twenty-six times.

The surviving members of the regiment continued to be actively engaged until the afternoon of the next day, when they withdrew and joined the march back to Corinth. In the two days of battle, their losses in killed, wounded, and missing was 500 men. Though the regiment would continue to fight for three more years, they were never the same after Shiloh. As Robert Gates, a member of the unit, put it, "The flower of the regiment was gone."

There are no markers at Shiloh in the scrub woods in front of the Hornet's Nest, where the unit was shattered. I like to walk there and think about the young soldiers who left their homes in West Tennessee only to die at Shiloh. Can you not see Colonel Stephens leading the brigades with the colors flying high and the soldiers behind, dressing their lines? And then, as they are cut down, the innocence of war is forever over.

Six months later, they lost ninety-one men at the Battle of Perryville. By December, their numbers were so low that it became necessary to combine the regiment with the 9th Tennessee, another West Tennessee regiment. At year's end, they fought at Murfreesboro. The combined regiments had 412 men, but suffered another forty-two casualties.

In the summer of 1863, 335 men were present at the Battle of Chickamauga, where half of the regiment was lost.

In November, after having taken part in the Battle of Missionary Ridge, they fell back to Dalton, Georgia, where they went into winter camp, having marched for sixty hours with only five hours of rest. The combined regiments had 329 men.

In 1864, the regiment was constantly engaged in the Atlanta Campaign, with their heaviest engagement at the famous "Dead Angle" at the Battle of Kennesaw Mountain. On the last day of November, they were a part of Cheatham's Division that stormed the Federal lines at Franklin. Every general or field officer in the division was killed or wounded, except one colonel. Following the Battle of Nashville, they were part of the rear guard action, which enabled the weakened army to retreat across the Tennessee River. In April of 1865, they were a part of General Joe Johnston's army, which surrendered at Greensboro, North Carolina. They were paroled on May 1, 1865.

It had been a long journey since that time when they loaded into wagons in May of 1861 to come to Jackson to become soldiers. Gone were the crowds who saw them off to war at the old Mobile and Ohio depot. Gone, too, were most of the soldiers. Of the 1,200 who left Jackson, only 100 or so were left to come home.

Today, the statue of a Confederate soldier stands in front of the courthouse, always facing north, as a reminder of the bravery of those young men. As long as the old soldiers were alive, they told their stories when gathered at their bivouacs. They are all gone—long gone—and it is up to us to remember their bravery and keep their stories alive.

Confederate Submarine Hunley

A Relic from Shiloh

Do you know the story of C.S.A. Lieutenant George E. Dixon? His life and death as a Confederate soldier and submarine commander is one of the most fascinating stories of the Civil War. Unlike most stories of long ago, the ending of this tale is still unfolding.

Dixon was a member of the 21st Alabama Infantry. His Alabama sweetheart was named Queenie Bennett, a young girl only fourteen years old. As a memento, when he was going away to war, she gave him a twenty-dollar gold piece, which he kept in his pocket.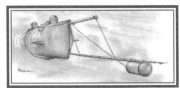

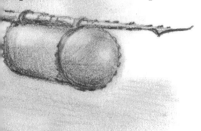

The 21st Alabama was a part of General Adley Gladdin's brigade along with three other Alabama regiments, the 1st Louisiana Infantry and a battery of artillery from Florida. Dixon and his comrades were among the first of the Confederate units to slam into the unsuspecting Federal camps at Shiloh early on the morning of April 6, 1862. Over a two-day period, they suffered losses of 198 killed, wounded, and missing, more than forty percent of the regiment.

George Dixon was one of the casualties, struck in the leg by a Yankee bullet. Remarkably, Dixon was unharmed, for the bullet hit the gold piece in his pocket, saving him from losing his leg and probably his life. To commemorate the event, Dixon had a jeweler polish and engrave the bent coin with these words:

Shiloh
April 6, 1862
My Life Preserver
G. E. D.

Now the scene shifts to Charleston, South Carolina, in February of 1864. Bombarded by land and blockaded by sea, the city where the opening shots of the war were fired was slowly strangling. To survive, the Union blockade had to be broken. To do so, Confederate commanders turned to a most improbable weapon—a submarine! Never before had an underwater ship been used to attack other ships. Seven years later, Jules Verne would publish his novel *Twenty Thousand Leagues Under the Sea*. But that was only a book—no one had really sailed a ship below the water's surface.

In the spring of 1863, a submarine was built in Mobile, Alabama, and shipped by train to Charleston. It was named the *Hunley* for one of the designers. For two weeks, the *Hunley* made nighttime voyages from the harbor in hopes of sinking a Yankee ship, but without success. Impatient, the city authorities took the ship over and manned her with a crew of eight sailors and a new captain. The *Hunley*, with its inexperienced crew, sank, killing five of the nine men. It was raised, repaired, and remanned. Six weeks later, it sank again, killing the crew of seven sailors and its designer, Horace Hunley. Sailors along the waterfront began to refer to the *Hunley* as "the murdering machine" and joked that "it would sink at a moment's notice and at times without it!"

One of the engineers who worked on the project was Lieutenant George Dixon, the same George Dixon who had miraculously survived at Shiloh when his gold coin deflected a Yankee bullet. With Horace Hunley dead, Dixon appealed to General Beauregard to let him pilot the boat. At first, Beauregard refused, saying, "I can have nothing more to do with that submariner boat. Tis more dangerous to those who use it than to the enemy." Eventually, Beauregard relented and allowed Dixon to take command of the boat with eight other volunteers who wanted to be first in history to engage an enemy ship in this manner. Beauregard required that all volunteers be made aware of the hazard involved, saying, "If the submarine didn't kill them, the Yankees would be happy to oblige." Admiral John Dahlgren, commander of the Union blockade, had received rumors of some type of underwater boat and responded that captured submariners deserved to be hanged "for using an engine of war not recognized by civilized nations."

Commanders of the Yankee fleet were now aware of the Confederate submarine presence, tipped off by Rebel deserters. In response, the Federal ships operating within the harbor used an elaborate screen of metal chains to keep any underwater attackers away. Deprived of these close-in targets, Dixon was forced to concentrate on targets outside of the harbor, ten to twelve miles from shore.

Night after night, the *Hunley's* crew of eight squeezed into their claustrophobic vessel. Sitting shoulder to shoulder on a wooden bench, they hand-cranked the propeller. Attached to the front of the ship was a spar tipped with a deadly charge of black powder. Cranking for hours, they would get six to eight miles out to sea before turning around in order to reach shore before dawn, knowing they would be destroyed if they were discovered. This went on for over a month until the night of February 17, 1864, when a steam sloop, the U.S.S. *Housatonic,* anchored just four miles from shore. The *Hunley* slipped away from a dock on nearby Sullivan's Island just after sunset. Traveling about six feet below the surface of the water, they reached the *Housatonic* about 8:45.

John Crosby, acting master aboard the *Housatonic,* spotted something resembling a porpoise and gave the alarm. Sailors began firing at the object, but it was too late. The *Hunley* rammed her spar into the *Housatonic's* side, well below the waterline. Backing away, a trigger cord detonated the charge, blowing off the entire aft quarter of the ship. Within minutes, the ship sank, killing five sailors. The rest of the crew were rescued by other ships. This was the first time in history that a submarine sank an enemy warship. It was but the predecessor of what would come in later wars with Nazi U-Boats.

Confederates on Sullivan's Island reported seeing a signal—a blue lantern light that meant the *Hunley* was heading home—some forty minutes after the attack. But the *Hunley* never returned. What happened to George E. Dixon and his eight-man crew was a mystery for 131 years, until May of 1995, when a group of shipwreck hunters led by novelist Clive Cussler discovered the *Hunley* buried under three feet of silt in Charleston Harbor, only 1,000 feet from where the action occurred.

On August 8, 2000, the *Hunley* was raised after three months of work and at a cost of 2.7 million dollars. Now archeologists with the National Park Service are beginning to sift through the mud and silt inside the submarine. The location of every artifact and bone of the skeletonized crew is being mapped. The remains of each of the crew were still in their place. And at the front of the ship was the captain, George Dixon. As his skeleton was being prepared to be removed, the chief archaeologist, probing through the silt, felt the edge of a coin. It was the fabled twenty-dollar gold piece given to Dixon so long ago by his Alabama sweetheart. Who could write such a story of a gold coin? From the firestorm of Shiloh to a Confederate submarine at the bottom of the Atlantic, it reminds us still of the courage of a young soldier and a sweetheart to whom he never returned.

September 23, 1940
Tennessee National Guard
Troops Marching Off to War

Going Off to War

It is late winter in West Tennessee, and our young men, and women, too, are going away. Not only here, but also all across America, they are going away to war in Iraq. Regular army soldiers, as well as reservist and national guardsmen, are leaving families and jobs behind to fight a war on foreign soil. To do so is part of our culture. It is nothing new. The scene repeats itself generation after generation. But the price is painful to send family members away, to place them in harm's way, and emotions run high. Scenes of departure, as the troops prepare to leave, tear at our feelings. How long will they be gone, and will they return safely?—questions that have no answers.

In the Nashville, Chattanooga and St. Louis (NC & STL) Railroad Museum at the Jackson depot on South Royal Street, there is a picture that seems just the same as pictures on the front page of today's newspapers. This picture was taken more than sixty years ago on September 23, 1940, when the men and boys of the 117th Infantry Regiment of the 30th Division (National Guard) assembled at the Armory and then marched down South Royal to the NC & STL station. The unit in the picture is the medical unit that included Drs. Jack Thompson, Don Webb, and T. K. Ballard just as they reached the Murphy Hotel. Another picture shows a large crowd gathered around the train to say good-bye as they departed for Fort Jackson, South Carolina, for training. War had been declared in Europe, but America was not involved. Most people believed President Franklin D. Roosevelt when he promised that no American men or boys would be sent to foreign soil to fight a war. When their one-year term of enlistment was almost up, Congress passed a law to keep them on active duty. Two months later, the Japanese attacked Pearl Harbor. It would be five and a half years from the time they boarded the train in Jackson until they returned home.

A very similar scene occurred in Jackson in 1861, at the beginning of the Civil War. The 6th Tennessee Infantry was composed of 1,200 men from Madison, Fayette, Haywood, and Crockett counties. They received their initial training at Camp Beauregard where Airways Boulevard intersects with Hollywood Drive. On May 23, 1861, they received orders to proceed to Union City by train. Robert Gates, a member of the regiment, gave this description of the departure:

"There were very few men in the regiment over thirty-five years of age, and a large majority were under thirty. On Thursday, May 23rd, the regiment was ordered to be ready to leave for the front. On Sunday, May 26th, 1861, it left Jackson over twelve hundred strong for Union City, where an army was being concentrated to meet a probable invasion of Kentucky. The commanding officers endeavored to keep the day and hour of departure from the public, but in vain. The time became known on Saturday, and before the setting of the sun that day had spread all over the country. Sunday, May 16th, 1861 dawned bright and beautiful upon a scene that no tongue or pen may describe. An entire people had assembled—to say farewell, and bid God-speed to the brave boys who were the first of all the county to rally around The Southern Cross. Neither before nor since has Jackson looked on such a crowd as assembled to greet the Sixth Regiment on its departure for the seat of war. The line of march from the camp to the M. and O. depot, the distance of a mile and a half, was packed with people, the streets full, the houses covered, the very trees breaking with their human fruit.

Now and then a cheer would break forth as the regiment with difficulty made its way through the throng; but sobs and sounds of weeping, women screaming and fainting with mingled excitement and grief gave to that first march a wild and mournful character. At the depot a sea of humanity surged around the train upon which the regiment was embarking. There were acres of weeping women, shouting men, frantic girls and boys. Many fainted, many men and women went mad for the time, and over the troubled waves now and then would sweep a wail of grief, startling and unnerving. And of that twelve hundred or more who marched away to war on that memorable Sunday morning in May 1861, much less than half returned when the war was over. . ."

And so the soldiers march away, just as they have for decades past. And though we understand why they go, their departure is no less painful now than before. And as they leave, we are like those of long ago who watched the trains pull away and prayed for a safe and quick return.

Little Toy Cannons

Little Toy Cannons

In the late 1980s, a Civil War relic hunter, using a metal detector, found the campsite of the 11th Illinois Cavalry in Corinth, Mississippi. The ground was littered with bits of brick and tiny pieces of broken china. Dark stains on the ground were signs of old fire pits. In many cases, these fire pits contained items broken or discarded by the soldiers when the camp was abandoned in the summer of 1862. In one of the fire pits, the metal detector gave a strong signal of two buried objects. When the objects were uncovered, the digger found to his surprise two toy cannons, carved from lead. One is shorter than the other, just about one and a half inches long, and is a replica of a mortar. The other is four and a half inches long. If you look closely at the top of the larger one, there is a name etched into it. The name is Lavy S. Dusenberry.

After I had spent months researching, a faint image of Lavy Dusenberry began to emerge. The Illinois State Archives showed his name as Samuel Dusenberry, dropping his first name. He was from Pekin, Illinois, a small town near Peoria. He was a young man, just twenty-one years old, unmarried, and listed his occupation as a farmer. He was not very tall, standing just five feet six inches. But people were smaller then, and the muster roll for his company does not show anyone taller than five feet ten inches. He had brown hair, gray eyes, and a light complexion.

On September 21, 1861, Sam Dusenberry signed up for a three-year enlistment for his country. Surprisingly, he was mustered in as a sergeant, though he was younger than most of his company, Company F of the 11th Illinois Cavalry. (Three soldiers in Company F were still in their teens, the youngest being seventeen.)

I then wrote the National Archives in Washington to obtain his service record. When it finally arrived, it was something of a surprise. I had hoped that Sam Dusenberry was a hero with a good record of his years as a Civil War soldier. It did not turn out exactly that way.

Through March and April of 1862, Dusenberry is listed as a farrier (a blacksmith who shoes horses). He was still a sergeant during this time. However, on April 30, he apparently did something wrong and was reduced to the rank of private. From July through October, he distributed supplies in the Quartermaster Department before being assigned as an orderly for General Jeremiah Sullivan. He continued in this position until August 7, 1863, when he deserted the army and was not heard from again! The only notation on his record is that he owed the government one dollar and thirty-five cents for his belt buckle, which presumably he took with him.

I wonder what became of Sam Dusenberry. Did he just get tired and go home? I tried to track his descendants in his hometown of Pekin, Illinois. When I checked the telephone book there, to my surprise, I found a Sam Dusenberry listed. Hoping it might be a great-grandson, I called him. The man who answered was quick to tell me he never had an ancestor in the Civil War. Other efforts failed.

Though Sam Dusenberry is still something of a mystery, I know a lot more about him than when I started. Do you wonder why I was so interested in Sam Dusenberry? It is because I am the owner of those toy cannons, carved long ago by a young Illinois farmer turned soldier!

General William Hicks Jackson, C.S.A.
Supreme Court Justice Howell E. Jackson

Jackson's Jackson Family

Dr. Alexander Jackson was one of the first doctors to practice medicine in West Tennessee. In 1840, he moved his family to Jackson. His two sons, Howell E. Jackson and William Hicks Jackson, would become two of Tennessee's most distinguished citizens.

Howell Jackson was born in 1832. He graduated from West Tennessee College (now Union University) in 1848 and then studied at the University of Virginia for two years before returning to Jackson to read law with Judge A.W.O. Totten and Judge Milton Brown. In 1856, he graduated from law school in Lebanon and moved to Memphis where he practiced law until the beginning of the Civil War. As a strong member of the Whig party he was opposed to Tennessee seceding from the Union. When the war broke out, Jackson stayed

loyal to the South and served as receiver for sequestered property for West Tennessee.

Following the war, he returned to Memphis hoping to practice law. To do so, it was necessary to obtain a pardon for his service to the Confederacy. In 1866, his request was turned down by President Andrew Johnson. Eighteen months later, Johnson pardoned him, and he began to practice law again. Ironically, one of his first clients was Nathan Bedford Forrest, who expected to be indicted on civil and criminal charges from the war.

In 1874, he returned to Jackson to practice law with Alexander W. Campbell. Campbell, one of Jackson's most distinguished citizens, had served in the Confederate army, rising to the rank of general by the end of the war.

In 1880, Jackson was elected to the legislature. In 1881, though he did not want the office, he was elected to the United States Senate. Near the end of his term, he was appointed Circuit Judge of the United States Sixth Judicial District by President Cleveland. In 1891, he became the first judge of the Circuit Court of Appeals in Cincinnati when it was established. In 1893, he was appointed to the United States Supreme Court by President Benjamin Harrison. He is the only person in Jackson's history to serve as a justice of the Supreme Court.

Howell Jackson's younger brother, William Hicks Jackson, had a very different career. Like Howell, he attended West Tennessee College, but received an appointment to West Point, from which he graduated in 1856. When the Civil War broke out, he resigned his commission as a lieutenant of mounted riflemen and entered the Confederate service as a captain of artillery.

Known to his troopers as Billy or "Red," he was wounded at the Battle of Belmont. Upon recovery, he was appointed Colonel of the 7th Tennessee Cavalry. In late 1862, he was promoted to brigadier general, following the capture of Holly Springs. By the end of the war, he was in command of all the Tennessee cavalry under Nathan Bedford Forrest. Ironically, one of his division commanders was Alexander Campbell, who would later be his brother's law partner in Jackson. Jackson and Campbell are Jackson's only Confederate generals.

Three years after the war, Billy Jackson married Selene Harding, the daughter of General William G. Harding, owner of the Belle Meade Mansion near Nashville. He occupied himself for the rest of his life in the breeding and development of thoroughbred horses and in making Belle Meade one of the finest farms in the South.

Though the two brothers had followed different paths, circumstances brought them together again. In May of 1859, Howell had married Sophie Molloy, the daughter of a Memphis banker. In 1873, she died of consumption, leaving him to raise four children. Thirteen months later, he married General Harding's other daughter, Mary. Howell lived until 1895, dying in Nashville.

Though both brothers are buried in Middle Tennessee, they grew up in Jackson, and we claim them as our only Supreme Court justice and one of our two Confederate generals.

Sidewheeler Riverboat Sultana

Death on the Mississippi—
The Sultana

On the night of April 14, 1912, the *Titanic* steamed across the North Atlantic on her maiden voyage; she was the largest ship in the world—eleven stories high and 882 feet long. At 11:40 P.M., she struck an iceberg, opening a 300-foot gash in her hull. Several hours later, at 2:00 A.M., the *Titanic* went down. There were 2,227 passengers on board. Fifteen hundred and twenty-two of them lost their lives that night.

Surely you know all about the *Titanic*. Everyone is familiar with the story as a result of the movie, books, and traveling exhibition of artifacts brought up from the wreck by Bob Ballard. But have you ever heard of the *Sultana*? The *Sultana* was a wooden-hulled steamboat that exploded near Memphis at the end of the Civil War. Incredible as it may seem, the *Sultana* had more passengers than the *Titanic*, and more lives were lost. The explosion of the *Sultana* in 1865 still stands as the worst marine tragedy in American history. Yet few people know about it.

The *Sultana* had over 2,400 passengers on board. Its legal capacity was listed as 376! That was seven times the allowed number of people on board. The majority of the passengers were Union soldiers who had just been released from Confederate prisons. They were from Tennessee, Virginia, Indiana, Kentucky, Ohio, and Michigan. Many of the soldiers had been released from Cahaba Prison near Selma, Alabama. Most of those soldiers had been captured in September of the year before at Federal forts in Alabama, at Athens, and at Sulfur Branch Trestle, by Nathan Bedford Forrest. The remainder had been at Andersonville Prison near Americus, Georgia, having been captured at the battles of Franklin and Nashville. Chronic diarrhea, malnutrition, and scurvy plagued most of the soldiers. Many of them were little more than skeletons. James Brady of the 64th Ohio Infantry weighed 154 pounds when he entered Andersonville. When he was released, he weighed ninety-six pounds! William Peacock of the 9th Indiana Cavalry weighed 197 pounds when captured at Athens in September of 1864. When he boarded the *Sultana*, he weighed only ninety-one pounds! Despite this, an air of excitement surrounded them. After all of their hardships and misery, they were going home. Lt. William Dixon with the 10th Indiana Cavalry wrote:

"We were all talking of home and friends and the many good things we would have to eat. We considered ourselves lucky that we had lived through it and now we were in the land of the free. We had no thought but that we would be at home in a few days feasting with our loved ones once more."

In addition to the 1,866 prisoners, there were 100 passengers along with military guards and the boat's crew. The *Sultana* also carried a large store of freight, which included 250 hogsheads of sugar, each weighing 1,200 pounds, and ninety-seven cases of wine. On the main deck, there were 100 hogs and close to 100 mules and horses. But the strangest occupant on the boat was the crew's pet—a large alligator housed in a wooden crate!

The *Sultana* had been built in January of 1863 in Cincinnati for Captain Preston Lodwick, a prominent steamboat owner. The name *Sultana* refers to a Sultan's wife, sister, or mother. Three steamboats had previously carried this name, all of which had burned or sunk. Newspapers reported that the *Sultana* was one of the largest and best business steamers ever built and was ideally suited for trade on the Mississippi, Tennessee, and Ohio rivers. The steamer's cabin was a long narrow saloon flanked by staterooms on each side. The staterooms were luxuriously furnished and provided accommodations for seventy-six cabin passengers and 300 deck passengers.

The ship's captain was J. Cass Mason, a thirty-four-year-old riverman known to be one of the best pilots on the river. In March of 1864, Mason joined two other investors to purchase the *Sultana* from Captain Lodwick. By April of 1865, Mason was in financial trouble and had sold parts of his ownership to other investors. Mason's last asset was his equity in the *Sultana*. The army was paying five dollars per enlisted man and ten dollars for officers for the transportation of the prisoners. Mason needed to get as many prisoners as possible on board his ship.

At 9:00 P.M. on April 24, the *Sultana* backed away from the wharf at Vicksburg. Troops occupied every inch of space on the deck and roof of the boat. When the *Sultana* landed at Helena, Arkansas, a photographer decided to take a picture of the ship and all of the prisoners. When the passengers rushed to the side of the boat nearest the photographer, the ship very nearly capsized. The *Sultana* docked at Memphis at 6:30 P.M. on April 26, the same day John Wilkes Booth was killed. While the sugar and wine were being unloaded, many of the former prisoners left the ship and went into Memphis to celebrate their freedom at local saloons. The *Sultana* left Memphis at 11:00 P.M. and steamed across the river to Hopefield, Arkansas, where over 1,000 bushels of coal were loaded on.

By 2:00 A.M., the ship was seven miles north of Memphis, struggling against the current, but traveling at her normal speed of nine miles per hour. The weather was chilly with a light rain falling. Occasional flashes of lightning lit the night sky as the pilot maneuvered the ship through a series of islands known as Paddy's Hen and Chicks.

Without warning, three of the ship's four boilers exploded. The initial impact ripped the vessel in half, sending flames across the boat and releasing scalding steam, killing scores of people. Within twenty minutes, the entire length of the boat was on fire.

Believing they were near the shore, passengers began leaping into the river. Unfortunately, the river was at flood stage, more than four miles wide. The Sultana carried only seventy-six cork-filled life preservers and a metal lifeboat. So many people climbed into the lifeboat that it soon sank, along with its passengers. Others clung to any type of debris they could find.

William Lugenhead, a soldier with the 153rd Ohio Infantry, stabbed the pet alligator with his bayonet and threw the crate overboard for use as a raft. He was finally rescued three miles below Memphis, still clinging to the crate. Several soldiers were holding onto a log floating toward Memphis when a horse swam up to them in the dark and threw its head over the log. Thinking it was the alligator, they let go of the log and looked for something else to hold onto.

The first rescue boat, the *Bostonia No. 2*, was ninety minutes away when the crew spotted the glow of the burning ship. When they reached the *Sultana*, they found the river filled with dead or dying passengers. The *Bostonia*'s master, Captain John T. Watson, directed the crew to pitch anything that would float into the river, including tables, chairs, planks, and bales of hay. Time was running out for many of the malnourished soldiers. Some drowned while others died from hypothermia or exposure.

Steamboats docked at Memphis spread the news of the disaster by sounding their bells. The first light of morning brought the reality of the disaster. The dead seemed to fill the river both above and below Memphis. Naked and helpless men lay all along the levee, suffering from exposure, burns, and other injuries. Many soldiers hung from bushes or sat naked perched in trees.

Over 700 survivors were placed in Memphis hospitals, though nearly 300 of them later died. The recovery of bodies from the Mississippi continued for several weeks, with some victims being found as far south as Vicksburg. A week after the explosion, one crewmember of another boat reported seeing the body of a woman floating down river with a child in her arms. Most of the bodies were buried in Elmwood Cemetery in Memphis. In 1867, most of the military dead were moved to the newly established National Military Cemetery.

Stories of the tragedy soon disappeared from newspapers, leading some to suspect a cover-up by the War Department. It is more likely that other events, such as the end of the war or President Lincoln's assassination, caused people to forget it. Perhaps the nation had grown used to large numbers of war casualties, and yet the death of 1,800 people was greater than the loss on both sides at the Battle of Bull Run.

Secretary of War Edwin Stanton ordered a board of inquiry to look into the loss of the *Sultana*. After months of testimony, the case was closed. Those involved in the tragedy were exonerated.

Today, the loss of the *Sultana* is little more than a footnote in America's history. Yet it still stands as our greatest maritime tragedy. When you are in Memphis, stand on the bluffs overlooking the river. Look upstream and try to imagine what it looked like on the fateful night of April 27, 1865.

EMILY SUTTON
A VICTIM
OF
THE EPIDEMIC
DIED
OCT. 4, 1873

SUTTON

Emily Sutton Monument, Elmwood Cemetery

Flight from the Yellow Jack

It is the beginning of winter as I write this, and front-page headlines warn of a flu epidemic—or worse, a worldwide epidemic known as a pandemic. As frightening as flu epidemics may sound, it bears little comparison to epidemics of past years. Go to any of our older cemeteries and look at the headstones that tell the story of many of our ancestors who died at an early age. Especially sad are the markers for the children.

Since the arrival of the Pilgrims there have been nine different epidemics of measles. Other epidemics of influenza, cholera, and smallpox have taken their toll. The four great cholera epidemics were spread by immigrants from Europe, but by 1890, the disease was practically controlled. During World War I, more people were hospitalized from influenza than from wounds. In some training camps, there was an eighty percent death rate. Malaria and tuberculosis sickness reached epidemic proportions in the late 1880s. Yellow fever, or yellow jack, as it was called, was the one health hazard Southerners feared most. What the bubonic plague had been to medieval Europe, yellow fever was to West Tennessee and the Mississippi Delta.

The disease caused fevers, chills, hemorrhaging, severe pains, and sometimes a jaundicing of the skin, which gave yellow fever its name. The trademark of the disease was the victims' black vomit, composed of blood and stomach acids. The disease was transmitted from person to person by the female mosquito. Most likely, it was brought in by sailors on ships from the Caribbean or West Africa to New Orleans, where it was transmitted to the local population. Memphis was first exposed to the disease in 1828, then again in 1855 and 1867, but nothing prepared them for what would occur in the 1870s.

In August of 1873, the steam tug *Bee*, out of New Orleans, stopped in Memphis to let off two passengers who were ill. In a short time, both of them died of yellow fever, though few people noticed. By September 17, the Board of Health was forced to admit that yellow fever was epidemic. Panic ensued, and more than half of the town's white population fled the city. Of the 15,000 who remained, a third were sickened and 2,000 died.

To make matters worse, a national financial panic erupted as the 1873 epidemic ended. Banks closed throughout the country. In Memphis, Nathan Bedford Forrest's plans for a railroad line into Alabama failed, forcing him into bankruptcy. Another casualty was Jefferson Davis, who lost the last of his money, forcing him to leave his wife, Varina, in Memphis while he sought opportunities elsewhere.

Yellow fever did not reappear for five years until a mild winter, a long spring, and a hot summer produced ideal conditions for breeding mosquitoes and the spread of the disease. News of yellow fever raging in the West Indies reached Memphis on June 3. Inquiries to New Orleans and Mobile produced negative responses, but by late July, New Orleans newspapers reported an epidemic in progress. By July 30, terrified residents of Grenada, Mississippi, began streaming into Memphis with reports of sickness and death. Memphis officials attempted to quarantine the city by posting officers at all of the major roadways. It was too little, too late. On August 13, the first death was recorded in Memphis. With memories of the 1873 epidemic still fresh on their minds, a panic ensued. Twenty-five thousand residents fled the city, leaving a population of 12,000 blacks and only 6,000 whites behind. Trains leaving the city were so crowded that passengers were hanging out of the windows. Some who could not obtain a ticket boarded anyway with the aid of drawn pistols.

Over ninety percent of the whites that remained contracted the fever, and seventy percent of them died. The disease raged until the first frost came on October 19. Over 17,000 people were infected, and 5,150 of them died. Though the black population contracted the disease as quickly as the whites, only seven percent of those infected died. Repeated exposure over many years in West Africa had apparently helped to build up immunity to the disease.

Dr. William Ramsey wrote:

"No words can describe the filth I saw, the rotten wooden pavements, the dead animals, putrefying human bodies and the half-buried dead combining to make the atmosphere something fearful. 'The city is almost depopulated,' wrote a policeman in September. 'The death rate is over one hundred every day. The undertakers can't bury them fast enough. We find a lot that have been dead three or four days. My God it is fearful.' As the death toll rose to more than a hundred a day, carpenters doubled the price of wooden coffins, but still could not make them quickly enough. Pans of sulphur burned in the halls of the Peabody Hotel. Entire families died leaving no one to dispose of their property."

From this chaos, a remarkable character emerged. Her name was Annie Cook (at least that was what she called herself). She was an attractive woman of German descent who was the madam of the Mansion House, an upscale brothel on Gayoso Street. When the 1873 epidemic struck, she dismissed her guests and opened the house for patients. Five years later, when the yellow jack struck again, she repeated her charitable acts, but this time, she too became ill and died of the fever on September 11.

Her obituary the next day in *The Memphis Daily Appeal* read in part:

> *"Annie Cook, the woman who, after a long life of shame, ventured all she had of life and property for the sick, died Sept. 11, of yellow fever, which she contracted while nursing her patients. If there was virtue in the faith of the woman who but touched the hem of the garment of the Divine Redeemer, surely the sins of this woman must have been forgiven her. Her faith hath made her whole—made her one with the loving Christ, whose example she followed in giving her life that others might live."*

She is buried in Historic Elmwood Cemetery in the Howard Association lot. (The Howard Association was organized in New Orleans in 1853 to provide aid for yellow fever victims, with a Memphis chapter being organized in 1855. The members wore yellow armbands to identify themselves as they distributed food and medicine. Ten of them died in the 1878 epidemic.) Nearby is the statue of another madam, Emily Sutton, who died in the 1873 epidemic. Like Annie Cook, she too abandoned her profession and died while caring for the sick. Close to these markers is an area designated as "No Man's Land," where 1,500 yellow fever victims are buried in four public lots.

Another yellow fever marker is for four Episcopal nuns who ran the St. Mary's Episcopal School and the Church Home for Orphans. Of the thirty children in the Church Home, all but four came down with the fever and twenty-two died. All four of the nuns died within days of each other and have a common headstone. They are buried at right angles to form the shape of a cross. In 1985, the General Convention of the Episcopal Church designated them as the Martyrs of Memphis.

Long after the epidemic was over, Memphis continued to feel its effects. The financial position of the city was in such dismal condition that the legislature revoked the city charter in 1878. The disease was even worse in other West Tennessee towns. Germantown, Moscow, Milan, Collierville, Paris, Brownsville, Martin and LaGrange experienced staggering losses relative to the size of their populations. The fever even spread to Chattanooga, causing 8,000 of the residents to flee.

Fortunately, Jackson, Tennessee, just eighty miles east of Memphis, did not suffer as much as its neighboring communities. On August 12, having learned of the spread of the fever from New Orleans to Memphis, four physicians and the mayor, W. D. Robinson, organized a Board of Health. Immediately, they initiated quarantine against Memphis, New Orleans, and Grenada, Mississippi.

Each afternoon, when the courthouse bell rang, squads of armed young men assembled to guard the ten roads leading into town. Trains were stopped at the county line to get the mail and fumigate it. Papers and letters were put in ovens and baked on the assumption that the heat would kill the germs. Letters were perforated with many holes and vapors blown into the envelopes.

Due to the belief that the germ floated around more at night than in the day, large fires were lit to drive the yellow jack out. Mounds of mud-covered pinecones twenty to thirty feet high were constructed throughout the city. The smoke from the fires helped to drive the mosquitoes away, even though the people who lit the fires had no idea that the mosquitoes were the carriers of the disease. Strict enforcement of the quarantine laws and the use of lime and carbolic acid as disinfectants helped to control the disease. Even so, twenty-two people in Jackson contracted the yellow fever, all of whom died.

Three years later in 1881, Carlos Finlay, a Cuban physician, suggested that mosquitoes carried the disease. Walter Reed, a U. S. Army doctor, later proved that mosquitoes carried it, though a vaccine to prevent it was not developed until 1937. Today, yellow fever is forgotten as a life-threatening disease. Few people know or remember how the yellow jack could cause entire towns to flee or panic.

Highland Park, Jackson, Tennessee

Jackson's Highland Park

Who can imagine that there was once an amusement park located between Crescent and Westwood and bordered by Campbell. The park was named Highland Park. Today, the area is a quiet residential neighborhood, and the only thing left of the park is Campbell Lake. The park was developed by the Jackson and Suburban Railway Company and was accessible by streetcar from most major points in the city. Built at the turn of the century, it was the center of Jackson's social life from the "Gay Nineties" to the early 1920s.

Part of the park was Gorman's Field, a large baseball park. Jackson was a charter member of the Kentucky-Illinois-Tennessee (KITTY) League formed in 1903. Jackson's team, the Railroaders, opened the season there before a crowd of 500. Jackson was different then, and attempts to play on Sunday afternoons met with disapproval and a court order forbidding it. The league lasted only a year but started again in 1910. Jackson's team, renamed the Climbers, played their opening game at the park before a crowd of 2,000.

In the amusement park was a white stucco building called the Temple of Winged Feet, which, of course, was a skating rink. Nearby was a refreshment parlor called the Polar Bear. For thrills, there was a real roller coaster.

On the lake, there was a beautiful white stucco bridge for couples to stroll across while others boated on the lake. Near the lake was a pavilion where band concerts were held on Sunday afternoons.

Both local and touring professional groups played in the pavilion there. In 1898, the Mikado was performed using local talent. Emma Inman Williams, in her book *Historic Madison*, listed a crowd of 10,000 people in attendance for *The Last Days of Pompeii*. If this number is correct, it would be one of the largest crowds ever gathered in Jackson.

When you next drive down Campbell, look over at the lake and try to imagine what it must have once been. Little is left today but the memories.

Highland Park, Jackson, Tennessee

Marathon Automobile

The Marathon Automobile

On July 31, 1985, Governor Lamar Alexander announced that a new General Motors Company—Saturn—would build a giant industrial plant in Spring Hill, a small town thirty miles south of Nashville. Located in northern Maury County, Spring Hill had only recently passed the 1,000 population mark. General Motors created the Saturn Corporation to compete against continued increases in Japanese imports.

The name was derived from the Saturn space project that sent the United States to the moon ahead of the Soviet Union. The site covered 2,400 acres and housed a 4.3 million square-foot factory. It changed Spring Hill forever. Farms and homes sold at spectacular prices.

Some people began to refer to Tennessee as "Detroit South" after the Saturn announcement. But was this something new or history repeating itself? Many would be surprised to learn that Jackson and Nashville had a chapter in American automobile history that dates back more than ninety years.

The Southern Engine and Boiler Works Company started business in Jackson in 1874. Two mechanics named Sherman and Cole created the business by opening a small shop on the corner of Lexington and M & O Railroad. They began by building small engines and boilers. As the business prospered, they sold their shop to local stockholders who selected Exile Burkett to be manager. The company continued to expand and prosper, so much so that a new plant was built at 334 to 354 North Royal, across the street from the original location. This new plant occupied three acres. By 1900, 400 people were working there making high-pressure boilers, steam engines, and sawmills and also operating a casting works.

The first mechanical engineer to be hired was W. H. Collier, who designed their first Corliss steam engines, which were built in units of 100 to 300 horsepower. At the turn of the century, the company was the largest business in Jackson.

Collier, who started as an apprentice, designed a gasoline engine to be used in sawmills. (This was just one of eight potentially successful inventions.) By 1906, Collier had convinced his supervisors that the gasoline engine could be used in the newest craze sweeping the country, the automobile! W. H. Collier designed and Southern Engine and Boiler Works manufactured the first automobile made in the South! Other companies in the South made automobiles, but Southern Engine and Boiler Works is credited with being the first because they made the cars from scratch. All parts of the car were made in the plant. Initially, the cars were named the Southern. The discovery of another automobile also called Southern led Collier to change the name to Marathon. The name Marathon was selected from names submitted in a contest to name the car by a girl who was a student at Jackson High School. The symbol for the new name was a Roman runner. Later, the company named three of its other models the Runner, the Winner, and the Champion to capitalize on the 1912 Olympic Games.

Between 1906 and 1910, approximately 600 cars were made in Jackson. The two models, a rumble seat roadster and a five-seat touring car, sold for $1,500. Despite their apparent success, the Southern Engine and Boiler Works never made a strong effort to promote the car. Perhaps they were too successful with their main line of products to worry with something as new as the automobile. Or perhaps they did not realize where America was headed with these temperamental, noisy machines.

In 1910, a group of investors purchased the Marathon and moved it to Nashville. Augustus H. Robinson, a banker, real estate developer, and owner of the Maxwell House Hotel, led the group. The purchase price was $400,000 for the rights to make the car, as well as the equipment to manufacture it. Most importantly, W. H. Collier, the inventor and designer, was part of the package.

The new company purchased a plant facility at 1200 Clinton Avenue. (Conveniently enough, Robinson already owned the property.) The line expanded to five models in 1911 and to twelve models on four chassis by 1913. The workforce grew from seventy-five to 400. The production rate rose to 200 cars monthly, with predictions of 5,000 cars annually, and for a short while, the future looked very bright. In one monthly period, twenty Marathon models were sold, compared to two General Motors cars, two Packards, and one Buick. In 1911, a local Marathon dealership opened for business at 1205 Broadway.

Having so many models to choose from seemed to confuse customers. As a contrast, Ford made only one model from 1907 to 1926—the Model T. Rolls Royce made only the Silver Ghost for the same twenty-year period. Successful automakers seemed to concentrate on only one model and marketed it successfully to the public.

Collier disagreed with the company president in 1913 and was demoted. Marathon had three new presidents in four years. Collier filed charges of mismanagement, suppliers filed claims for unpaid invoices, and in 1914, Marathon stopped building cars. The company continued to manufacture parts until 1918. After that, it faded into obscurity.

Southern Engine and Boiler Works grew to be one of the biggest of its kind in the South, until changing technology spelled its doom as the popularity of oil engines and electric power increased. It went out of business in 1926.

W. H. Collier lost everything when Marathon failed. In Jackson, he is best remembered for The Cedars, the home he built on Cotton Grove Road on the site where Adam Huntsman's house once stood. Just west of the house was a lake, a popular recreational spot during the 1920s and 1930s, known as Collier's Lake. Collier's Lake dried up long ago, and The Cedars has had many owners. Southern Engine and Boiler's buildings on North Royal Street still stand as a memorial to a time when automobiles were manufactured in Jackson, Tennessee.

Woodland Baptist Church

Pillars of Faith

As the early settlers moved into Tennessee, they built churches, almost as quickly as they built their homes. The lives of the communities centered around their churches. Some of the men who would fill the pulpits were very colorful; others were very powerful. Isaac Lane was a former slave who started a college. Mark Matthews helped to start a library, a milltown, a school, and a hospital. Obadiah Dodson preached on riverboats on the Hatchie River while wearing a yellow bandana tied on his head.  Howell Taylor came from Virginia and started a Methodist campground that thrives today. There were many like them, but these four were exceptional. They were "pillars of faith."

Bishop Isaac Lane

Isaac Lane was born as a slave on March 4, 1834. He was one of twenty-seven slaves on the plantation of Cullen Lane, five miles east of Jackson. He was well-treated by his owner and taught himself to read and write. In 1853, Lane married Frances Ann Boyce, a slave woman from Haywood County. The couple had twelve children, many of whom became ministers, educators, or physicians. The Civil War ruined his master, Cullen Lane, financially, and Lane died in poverty. So that his former master might have a proper funeral, Isaac Lane purchased the books in his library.

On December 15, 1870, the Colored Methodist Episcopal Church was organized in Jackson by the General Conference of the Methodist Episcopal Church South. The first official CME Church was known as "Mother Liberty." (In 1954, the name was changed to Christian Methodist Episcopal Church.) Lane quickly gained in stature in the growing congregation, and in 1872, he was elected a bishop.

In 1882, he established a CME school in Jackson to provide education for freedmen (former slaves). His daughter, Jennie Lane, became the first principal and teacher. When the school applied to become a college, Lane chose a white Methodist minister to be its first president. In 1907, Bishop Lane's son, James Franklin Lane, became president of Lane College and continued to serve in that capacity for 37 years.

During World War II, the United States named a Merchant Marine victory ship in his honor, the U.S.S. *Lane,* based in San Diego. It is the only World War II victory ship still in service. Bishop Isaac Lane died in 1936 at the age of 102.

Mark Matthews—The Black-Maned Lion of Seattle

Perhaps the most extraordinary minister to occupy the pulpit of Jackson's Presbyterian Church was Dr. Mark Allison Matthews. He was born in Calhoun, Georgia, in 1867 into a family whose business and home had been destroyed by General Sherman in the Civil War.

He was licensed to preach in 1886 and ordained in 1887. His first call was to Calhoun, Georgia. Besides being pastor there, he visited five other rural churches every Sunday. From Calhoun, he accepted a call to Dalton, Georgia, but left there for Jackson in 1896. Not yet thirty when he began his ministry in Jackson, Matthews possessed a brilliant mind and was a forceful, imposing speaker. He stood six feet five inches in the pulpit.

The characteristic that set him apart from previous ministers was the number of civic projects that he helped develop for the city. Some of his projects included:

* Establishing Presbyterian Night School for working people. Within four years, the number of teachers had increased to thirty-five and more than 600 students had passed through the school.
* Leading the fight to persuade Andrew Carnegie to donate $30,000 for the building of the Carnegie Library and persuading the City Council to purchase a lot for it and provide maintenance funds.

- Leading the church in establishing the Presbyterian Hospital in 1897. He secured Dr. Jere L. Crook as its first administrator and served as its first president.
- Beginning the process of establishing a YMCA by selecting a site and helping to begin its operation.
- Helping to raise money for the purchase of land for the Bemis Cotton Mill to entice them to locate to Jackson in 1900.
- Organizing the Humane Society in 1897 to publicize the need for prevention of animal and child abuse.
- Organizing the Ladies Bible Training School, whose members identified 750 people a year in need of clothing, food, and fuel.
- Receiving 600 new members into the church during his pastorate.

Matthews left Jackson to become the minister of the First Presbyterian Church of Seattle in 1902, the largest congregation in the denomination at that time. His ministry spanned nearly forty years in the Pacific Northwest. In 1912, *Collier's* magazine described him as the "Black-Maned Lion of Seattle" when he was elected as moderator for the Presbyterian General Assembly. Further, the article states:

"Matthews had caught a large part of the nation with his evangelized efforts and his involvement with Seattle city politics. The man is a born troublemaker, a congenital disturber of the peace. He troubles his

town, he troubles his church, he troubles himself. He can never let well enough alone. He is the best-hated, most feared man in Seattle. But also he is the most loved."

Obadiah Dodson

One of the most picturesque characters of the early days in West Tennessee, Dodson was a Baptist minister and farmer. He was born in Halifax County, Virginia, in 1792. He moved with his wife to Middle Tennessee in the autumn of 1822. Three years later, he moved to West Tennessee. He felt called to preach the Gospel and began doing so in 1819. Endowed with a great deal of energy, he presented the subject of religion to people wherever he found them, whether in the home, on the road, or at church. By the time of his death, he had baptized nearly 5,000 people.

He was described as being very affable and courteous. He always wore a yellow bandanna handkerchief. He was a short man, about five feet seven inches in height, described as not having a very attractive appearance. He was bald-headed, with a narrow fringe of sandy hair. When he took his hat off, he usually pulled his bandanna over his head. He rode about the countryside on a sorrel horse and wore a white fur hat. When the hat was new, he looked very distinguished, but when the hat was old, he looked like a gristmiller. Appearances seemed to matter little to him; he was too preoccupied with preaching. Not scholastic but well read, he encouraged parents to educate their children. The author of a book entitled *Moral*

Instructor and Guide to Youth; A Book Containing Answers to Eleven Biblical Questions and also Seventeen Propositions upon the Training of Children, he was probably the first person in Madison County to be published.

During the winter months, when the Hatchie River was high, the steamboats ran from Memphis to Bolivar. The boats carried large crowds on Sundays. On one occasion, a passenger proposed that they have some preaching, as there were several preachers aboard. The preachers all declined, save for Dodson. As he began, a number of gamblers began laughing at him. He opened the service singing a familiar hymn:

> *"I'm on my journey home,*
> *I'm on my journey home,*
> *To the New Jerusalem,*
> *so fare you well."*

After the hymn, he bowed in prayer. Others began to pray with him. He then preached about the uncertainties of life and what should happen if the boat sank. Thereafter, he became a familiar face, as he preached frequently on the Hatchie. Times have changed. Can you imagine a steamboat on the Hatchie with a preacher wearing a bandanna on his head?

Reverend Obadiah Dodson planted more churches than any other minister of his day. He never met anyone, whether stranger or friend, to whom he did not present the Gospel. One of the churches he started was Brown's Creek Baptist Church. In 1835, the church split into two groups over the growing missionary movement. One group formed the Brown's Creek Primitive Baptist Church, while the majority of the members organized the Brown's Creek Missionary Baptist Church and built a new church to the south on Brown's Creek with Obadiah Dodson as the preacher. The church had both black and white members. After the Civil War, the former slaves formed their own church. The white members deeded the property to them and built a new church building for themselves. In 1870, they changed the name to Woodland Baptist Church. In 1880, Woodland Academy was chartered and a new school building was constructed adjacent to the church. This church remains an active part of the Woodland community and in recent years has been placed on the National Historic Register.

R Brown

Tabernacle—Howell Taylor

Richard Taylor moved to Montgomery County, Tennessee, from Mecklenburg County, Virginia. On February 14, 1825, he moved to Haywood County, Tennessee, and purchased 765 1/2 acres of land. The following year, his father, Reverend Howell Taylor, as well Richard's four brothers and their families, moved to Haywood County.

Reverend Taylor bought 500 acres of land adjacent to that of his son Richard. Three of the brothers also bought land in the same area, while one brother, Edmund Taylor, purchased land in Fayette County and moved there.

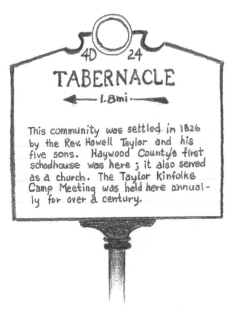

In the spring of 1826, the first church was built by Richard Taylor. It was a log building located in a grove of trees near his home. The church was named "New Hope." Soon after the church was completed, an addition was added so that the slaves could worship with them on Sunday and at the Wednesday night services. Howell Taylor was the first minister. On a three-acre tract, on a small hill overlooking the church, a cemetery was opened in 1829.

In 1832, a new church building was constructed some 400 yards distant from the first church. This also was a log building and was considered to be very fine. After the building was completed, the name was changed from "New Hope" to "Tabernacle" by Reverend Taylor, because the church where he had worshiped in Virginia was Tabernacle and he loved the name. The church was dedicated in 1832 by James Smith, a local preacher from Virginia.

Taylor Cemetery
at Tabernacle

Fifteen years later in 1847, a third building was constructed by James Thomas, a local carpenter. It was a white frame building with green shutters dedicated on October 3, 1847, by Reverend Guilford Jones. It lasted, with very little change, for seventy-five years, until it was remodeled and bricked in 1922. The chairman of the building committee was Harbert Thornton, a direct descendant of Reverend Howell Taylor. The church seats 340 people, though more may squeeze in on special Sundays.

The most special part of Tabernacle is the weeklong camp meeting held there. As the Tennessee historical marker on Highway 79 proclaims, "The Taylor Kinfolks Camp Meeting has been held here annually for more than a century." Originally, the meetings were daylong events. Then some of the families began to stay over in tents or wagons because of the travel time necessary to get there.

Soon, family camps replaced the tents. A camp consists of sleeping facilities surrounding a kitchen. To be considered a camp, the facility **must** have a kitchen. Some of the camps may have as many as fifteen sleeping rooms. The largest of the camps can sleep up to sixty people. For this many people, there are two dinner seatings. Each family has its own camp, kitchen, and cooks. Time and modern conveniences are beginning to change some of the traditions. The wood-burning stoves are being replaced by modern stoves. Coal oil lamps have given way to electricity, and running water has made buckets of well-drawn water a distant memory.

In the late 1950s, the first air-conditioning unit appeared. One Sunday, a preacher from Washington helped to raise enough money to air-condition the church.

In many ways, Tabernacle has changed. In many ways, it remains the same. The week spent there in mid-summer, with family members coming home from all over the country, is more popular than ever. There are thirty-seven camps now, and the old ball field may one day give way to new camps. The fried chicken, cakes, and pies, along with the late-night watermelon, are as good as ever. Young people still do their courting and get engaged at Tabernacle, in the cemetery.

Joe Thornton is president of the Taylors of Tabernacle Camp Meeting Association. He has held this position since 1967, a position he was appointed to even before he graduated from seminary. It is his duty to call people to prayer and church services by blowing on a ram's horn. This horn has been handed down through the years and has called generations of Taylors to church. It is a fitting symbol of the tradition the Taylors started long ago.

Taylor Cemetery at Tabernacle

Monroe Dunaway Anderson

Monroe Dunaway Anderson

Whats is the most frightening word you can think of? Many people would respond "cancer" without a second thought. And when cancer is mentioned, M.D. Anderson Hospital, Houston, Texas, is quickly identified with superior treatment of cancer and cancer research. Monroe Dunaway Anderson, for whom it is named, was born shortly after the end of the Civil War and died in 1939. Few people know anything about him. Even fewer people know he was born, grew up, and is buried in Jackson, Tennessee.

Monroe was one of eight children born to James Wisdom Anderson and his wife, Mary Ellen. He was named for his grandfather, William Monroe Dunaway, a Cumberland Presbyterian minister and Masonic Grand Master for Tennessee. Dunaway also served as mayor of Jackson and in 1873 was part of a group that formed the First National Bank of Jackson, serving as president until he died six years later. Monroe attended Southwestern Baptist University in Jackson (now Union University). Before he could complete his schooling, his uncle, Hu Anderson, asked him to accept a position at his bank, Peoples National Bank, as assistant cashier. He worked at Peoples National Bank for ten years, acquiring the nickname of the "Careful Cashier," a reputation that would accompany him throughout his lifetime. He was a meticulous dresser. Especially pleasing were the four-inch collars he wore with stylish cravats. A popular saying of the time was "four-inch collar and not a dollar." (Teasing him about being poor would not last very long.)

In 1904, he joined his brother, Frank, and Will Clayton in a partnership, Anderson Clayton and Company, a cotton merchandising and financing company. Each of the three partners put in $3,000 capital to start the company.

Will Clayton was also from Jackson, having moved there from Tupelo, Mississippi, in 1886. One of four children, Will dropped out of school when he was thirteen to help support the family. He studied shorthand and learned to use a typewriter; soon, he had a job as a court reporter. Three years later, he was in New York with the American Cotton Company! Regarded by his associates as an intellectual, he never went back to school, but taught himself and learned from the people with whom he was associated. He worked with the management and international operations of the American Cotton Company for eight years before leaving to help form Anderson Clayton and Company. A month after the company was founded, Will's younger brother, Ben, joined the group as a fourth partner. Ben was very similar to his older brother. Prior to his joining Anderson Clayton, he, too, had been an employee of the American Cotton Company in Houston.

Anderson Clayton and Company opened their first office in Oklahoma City in 1904. The first year, they handled 30,000 bales of cotton, making a profit of $10,000. The company made a profit of $60,000 in 1905 and 1906. By 1907, the partners began to look at Houston as the center of both rail and sea transportation for their cotton. They then asked Monroe to leave his job with Peoples National Bank in Jackson and open a Houston office.

Monroe Dunaway Anderson would remain in Houston for the next thirty-two years until he died in 1939. He never married, had few possessions, and lived in a hotel suite near his office. Anderson Clayton and Company grew and prospered through the years. By 1935, his interest in the company was worth $20 million. When he died, he was buried in the family plot in Jackson.

Anderson's partner, Will Clayton, would go on to even greater achievements in business and on the international scene. He served his country as Under Secretary of State and collaborated in writing the Marshall Plan at the end of World War II.

M. D. Anderson has been dead for sixty-five years, yet his name is more recognized today than during his lifetime. The term

M. D. Anderson Hospital is synonymous with the treatment of cancer and cancer research. Other places honor him by placing his name on libraries, auditoriums, classrooms, and even a planetarium at Lambuth University, all of which have benefited from his foundation. The largest of his endeavors, the Texas Medical Center, does not bear his name, yet without the contribution of a large part of his fortune, it would not exist.

When you next hear someone talking about cancer, think of cancer research and the hope that someday it will be cured. And remember M. D. Anderson, who, still today, is helping to make that possible.

The Sea Dragon—
Richard Halliburton's Chinese Junk

Sometimes I pretended I had a magic carpet, and without bothering about tickets and money and farewells, I'd skyrocket away to New York or to Rome, to the Grand Canyon or to China, across deserts and oceans and mountains. . .then suddenly come back home when the school bell rang for recess.

(*The Flying Carpet* by Richard Halliburton)

The Boy Who Lived Out His Dreams

Very few people recognize the name of Richard Halliburton. Though he has been dead for sixty-five years, he is still the epitome of romance and adventure for those who remember him. His exploits were featured on the front pages of newspapers around the world. Accounts of his adventures were translated into virtually every major language. As he traveled across the globe, he found himself in the company of Borneo headhunters, French Foreign Legionnaires, heads of state, Devil's Island convicts, and subscribers to the *Ladies' Home Journal.*

The 1920s and the 1930s were closing years for times of adventure and conquest. Halliburton's life and adventures were as colorful as could be imagined. Today, he is largely forgotten. His books are long since out of print. In his own way, he was a remarkable person. And for a decade and a half, he was the most famous Memphian in the world!

Just nine days into the twentieth century, he was born in January of 1900 in Brownsville, Tennessee, and lived there with his parents on Key Corner Street. Shortly after his birth, the family moved to Memphis. For a short time, he was a student at Hutchison School for Girls, where his mother was a teacher, before transferring to Memphis University School for Boys. When he was fifteen, he was sent to Lawrenceville Preparatory School in New Jersey, a preparatory school for Princeton. After graduation there, two years later, he entered Princeton with the class of 1921.

The summer of 1919 marked the beginning of his first big adventure. Bitterly disappointed that the World War in Europe had ended before he could participate, he made plans to run away. While his parents attended a house party in Mississippi, Richard was scheduled to spend the weekend with relatives in Brownsville. Instead, he went to New Orleans and signed on as an ordinary seaman on a freighter bound for England.

He spent the next eight months in France touring battlefields and walking about England and France, earning enough money for room and board by teaching English to French children. Returning to the United States, he resumed his studies at Princeton, graduating in 1921.

Determined to make literature his life profession, he set forth to travel across the world. On a second trip abroad, he left home with no money, believing the less money he had, the more he would earn. He was gone for two years traveling to the Matterhorn in the Alps, to Andorra in the Pyrenees Mountains, then to Gibraltar, Egypt, India, across the Himalayas into Tibet, to Siam, Angkor, China, Siberia, and Japan. Writing continuously, he supplemented his seaman's wages by writing articles for the *National Geographic, Asia,* and newspaper syndicates.

He returned to America in 1923 with a manuscript entitled *The Royal Road to Romance.* Nine publishers rejected it before the Bobbs-Merrill Company accepted it for publication. It was an immediate success, selling 100,000 copies in the first few months at five dollars per copy. Soon, it was translated into ten languages and became a best-seller throughout the world.

Now established as an author, he sailed off to Greece to retrace the travels of Ulysses as told in the *Odyssey.* To do so, he climbed Mount Olympus, ran the original Marathon, and swam the Hellespont, the first person to do so since Lord Byron. This trip resulted in a book called *The Glorious Adventure* that was as successful as his first book.

In 1928, Halliburton retraced Cortez's conquest of Mexico from Vera Cruz to Mexico City. Along the way, he dove into the Mayan Well of Death at Chichen Itzá, just to see how it felt to be a human sacrifice, and swam the entire fifty-mile length of the Panama Canal. (He was the first to do so.) He continued to Peru and Brazil, spent a summer with convicts on Devil's Island, and just like Robinson Crusoe, lived for a month on the island of Tobago. Stories of the Latin American trip appeared first in *Ladies' Home Journal* and then in book form with the title of *New Worlds to Conquer.* It sold nearly 40,000 copies in a month!

For his next adventure, Halliburton purchased an airplane, which he named "The Flying Carpet." With a pilot companion, he left California, flying eastward, for a two-year flight around the world. Highlights of the trip included flying across the Sahara Desert and spending a summer with the French Foreign Legion. On New Year's Day of 1932, they flew into Nepal and photographed Mount Everest, the first to do so from the air. From Singapore, in a plane fitted with pontoons, they flew to the island of Borneo and spent a month with the Dyak headhunters. These adventures were published in his fourth book, appropriately named *The Flying Carpet*. In 1935, the editors of fifty American newspapers sent Halliburton abroad and commissioned him to write a full-page story every Sunday for fifty-two weeks. With a circulation of nine million readers, most families in America could follow him from the Bahamas to Mecca. The highlight of the year was crossing over the Alps from Lake Geneva to Turin by way of the Great St. Bernard Pass on the back of an elephant, just as Hannibal did. These stories went into a book named *Seven League Boots*.

By 1937, Halliburton found himself the most widely read author in America, especially by young people. His next book, *Richard Halliburton's Book of Marvels,* was aimed directly at this audience. This book was so popular that he published a sequel the following year entitled *Richard Halliburton's Second Book of Marvels.* Seven hundred schools adopted these two books as geography textbooks.

In 1937, Halliburton began planning what would be his last adventure. It was from China to San Francisco on a Chinese junk, intending to arrive in time for the 1939 World's

Fair. The trip would be expensive, causing Halliburton to raise funds from friends and family and finally by placing a mortgage on his home. The Chinese junk was christened the *Sea Dragon*. It proved to be poorly designed and constructed and cost far more than expected.

The fourteen-man crew sailed from Hong Kong in February of 1939 but limped back into the harbor six days later for repairs and modifications. The *Sea Dragon* put to sea again on March 4. Nineteen days later, they sailed into a violent typhoon. The last radio message was received on March 19. The location was reported as 1,200 miles west of Midway Island near the International Date Line. No trace of the *Sea Dragon* or its crew was ever found.

Halliburton died as he lived, in the middle of adventure, going places, and doing things others only dreamed of. America mourned his death, and the 1939 World's Fair would not be the same without him. But perhaps it was time for him to go. The years of adventure and discovery were slipping away as America moved closer and closer to Pearl Harbor and another World War.

As a memorial to their son, Halliburton's parents gave the money to construct a beautiful collegiate Gothic bell tower on the campus of Southwestern (now Rhodes) College in Memphis. Today, the Richard Halliburton Memorial Tower reminds us of a boy who traveled to the farthest parts of the world seeking adventure.

Well, I'm grown up now. But as yet I haven't any son or daughter to go traveling with me. And so, in their places, may I take you.

(Richard Halliburton's *Complete Book of Marvels*)

German P.O.W. Camp

When the Germans Were Here

For years, the story has been told that the legendary German tank commander Erwin Rommel came through West Tennessee in the late 1930s, studying the campaigns of Confederate General Nathan Bedford Forrest. A restaurant near the Tennessee River used to have this story, along with other bits of local history, on their placemats. When he came through Jackson, he purportedly spent the night at a farmhouse on the Heidelberg Road. (What a great place for a German general to stay!) It is a wonderful rumor, but probably not true. In fact, Rommel's son explicitly denied that the Desert Fox ever came to America.

Lawrence Wells, a writer from Oxford, Mississippi, wrote a novel entitled *Rommel and The Rebel* about just such a visit. It was based on press accounts of five unnamed German soldiers who came to Mississippi prior to World War II. Even if Rommel never came here, others did—not as visitors, but as prisoners of war! During World War II, more than eleven million German soldiers were captured. About 3.8 million prisoners were in American custody, and of this number, 363,036 were sent to internment camps in the United States.

Most of the camps were set up in the South, where the mild climate reduced the cost of housing. Further, the isolated locations reduced the danger of sabotage or escape. The camps were provided with double barbed wire fences. Searchlights and machine-guns were atop the watchtowers. Lodging usually consisted of tents or wooden buildings similar to the quarters provided on American army bases.

Germans sent to the United States were the most fortunate of the P.O.W.s. America, even though times were hard, was not directly affected by the war. You can only imagine how their comrades in Russia were treated. Many of the prisoners were soldiers of the "Afrika Corps" who were captured in Tunisia in 1943, or prisoners from the Western Front after the invasion of 1944. Texas had more camps than any other state. In the Mid-South, thirty-one camps were located in Arkansas, seventeen in Mississippi, and seven in Tennessee. Of the Tennessee camps, three were in West Tennessee: One was in Memphis at the Defense Depot, one in Jackson at McKellar Field, and one at Camp Tyson near Paris.

German prisoners were sent to Tennessee because of the need to relieve a labor shortage. With so many young men away in Europe and the Pacific, the cotton industry was desperate for laborers. Prisoners began arriving in Memphis in late summer of 1944. By August, 600 P.O.W.s were there. By November, the president of the National Cotton Council asked for 5,000 laborers to help move the cotton crop. On November 8, the War Department authorized the use of 7,000 prisoners in sixteen states.

On November 11, 1944, *The Jackson Sun* reported that Jackson would have to house prisoners if they were to work here. The only alternative was the state penitentiary at Ripley. On January 23, the paper reported "War Department May Locate Prison Labor at Jackson." The next day, *The Jackson Sun* reported:

"Prisoners of war will be quartered at Kenneth D. McKellar Airport in the near future," it became known here today; with the contingent of 250 expected when the camp is opened.

These men will be used to help relieve the growing shortage in farm labor, the information states harvesting crops such as strawberries, tomatoes, cabbage, cotton and others for which there is not enough local labor.

Should the demand warrant, the local group of prisoners of war will be increased to 400 according to present plans.

Quarters will be prepared for prisoners and the supervisory personnel in buildings previously used by the primary school for aviation cadets. The buildings were erected by the Defense Plant Corporation on a tract of ground belonging to the federal government, contiguous to the airport proper."

As a contrast to the prison facilities awaiting the Germans was another article on the front page of the same paper describing the finding of Japanese prison camp O'Donnel in the Philippines, where 40,000 Americans and Filipinos died! Two weeks later on February 8, the first prisoners arrived in Jackson as reported in *The Jackson Sun*:

"The war came to Jackson and West Tennessee's doorstep today with the announcement of the arrival of 18 of the approximate 200 war prisoners at McKellar Field to be used in farm and perhaps cotton compress work. The prisoners are barracked at McKeller Field under the supervision of the War Department and will work on nearby farms under guard."

The next day, 185 more arrived, coming from Camp Forrest in Middle Tennessee. Three days later, on Monday, February 12, 200 prisoners were working eight-hour days on farms in Madison, Haywood, and Gibson counties.

Most of the prisoners were between eighteen and twenty years old. Many could speak English. Though they were prisoners under guard in a foreign land, they were safe from harm, unlike many of their comrades who would not survive the war. They were paid eighty cents a day, which came to about twenty-five dollars a month. As a comparison, in 1941, an American Army private was making twenty-one dollars a month. Most of the prisoners found they had more money than they could spend. A package of cigarettes cost thirteen cents. Soap was fifteen cents a bar, and Goldcrest beer was available for ten cents a bottle. Apple pie cost a dime a slice, and for the first time, many of them tasted pumpkin pie.

Picking cotton proved to be hard work for the Europeans. The weather was hot, the humidity was high, and there were lots of mosquitoes. To earn the eighty cents per day, a prisoner had to pick 150 pounds of cotton. If they picked more than the required quota, they sold the extra to other field hands. German officers were segregated into separate groups and were not allowed to work. As a result, they were not able to earn spending money as the enlisted men did.

Edwin Pelz was a German radio operator who watched American paratroopers jump into France on D-Day. Two weeks later, he was captured at Cherbourg. For Pelz, life as a P.O.W. at the Memphis Defense Depot was relatively easy until May 9, 1945, when the war in Europe ended. Thirty years later, Pelz still remembered it clearly:

"It was about noontime, the prisoners were told to come back to the camp from different places where they had worked. The camp commander and his staff appeared. For the first time in many months, guards surrounded us with rifles. Then we were told the news: Germany had surrendered. The war was over. At the P.O.W. camp, some of us cried, glad that the war was over. I was sad.

I don't know why. The friends I had lost in Europe came into my mind. The hard winters in Russia came into my mind. All the fears and all the tears. It was all good for nothing. Now that the war was over, rather than prison life getting easier, it got tougher. The change came when Red Cross officials discovered what prison life in Germany had been like for captured American soldiers. The Red Cross didn't care for us anymore. Before the surrender they had checked the camps every two or three months. But not after the 9th of May. Our canteen was emptied of all the stuff and we were put on 1,200 calories a day. They told us it was the same as the American prisoners in Germany had gotten."

Even though the U.S. government cut back on rations, the people of Memphis continued to express concern for the prisoners and slipped them sandwiches. In time, it was the farmers who were paying the workers who complained they didn't want them weak from hunger. It was not until Christmas of 1945 that rations reached their previous levels.

As the war wound down and soldiers began to return home from Europe, the German prisoners in the Mid-South were not released. In 1946, the repatriation of 14,000 soldiers was postponed at the request of the Secretary of Agriculture so they could help work the farms. One American soldier from Jackson, Grady Montgomery, returned home from a German prison camp to find German P.O.W.s working on his family's farm.

When the prisoners first entered the camps, they were watched very closely by their guards. As the months wore on, the guards began to relax since no one tried to escape. After all, where would they go? Then in January of 1946, the unexpected happened in Beulah, Mississippi. On the night of January 2, Lieutenant Helmet Von der Aue, a handsome Luftwaffe pilot, escaped with Mrs. Joseph R. Rogers, whose husband owned a 1,000-acre plantation where the Germans had been working. After four days, the FBI caught the couple in Nashville. Mrs. Rogers, an attractive thirty-seven-year-old brunette, was charged with aiding and abetting the escape and transporting an enemy of the United States. During testimony, Mrs. Rogers said she and Von der Aue had fallen in love and planned to get married. She gave her German lover some of her husband's clothes, and they drove away in his car. She denied being a German sympathizer, saying it was "an affair altogether of the heart." She received a two-year suspended sentence, and her German sweetheart was returned to his camp in Mississippi. Though she later divorced her husband, nothing further came of her German romance.

Fritz Schweigler, a German prisoner at Camp McCane (Grenada, Mississippi) had humorous memories of the way they were "guarded": "One time a guard fell asleep while we were working in the fields. We took his submachine gun apart. When he woke up he couldn't get it back together again. We only put it back together for him after he gave us all cigarettes. Another time a guard deserted while he was supposed to be watching us. He left his rifle there. When the day was over and we formed up to march back into camp, I slung the rifle over my shoulder and marched the group back into camp like I was the guard. The Americans didn't know what to say. It was so funny."

In March of 1946, the prisoners began their trip home. Although the prisoners thought they were going home, this was not the case. Most of the prisoners ended up in England, where they worked on farms and in mines until they were finally released in August 1948. For them at last, the war was finally over.

As the prisoners grew older, many of them grew nostalgic about their time in the United States. One Jackson prisoner was so changed by the experience that he returned to Germany and became a priest.

In June of 1975, Edwin Pelz returned to Memphis, thirty-one years after coming there as a P.O.W. The visit was made possible by local donations after *The Commercial Appeal* ran a series of articles in which Pelz told of his affection for the people of Memphis and the Mid-South. The article from the June 28, 1975, *Commercial* described his emotions at coming back:

"Pelz returned yesterday to West Germany—convinced that Memphis is the friendliest city in the world yet newly aware of man's inability to truly return to an earlier part of his life. 'The place and the people are the same,' he said, 'but the feelings are different because I was a young man, then, and I am no longer young. It is hard when you realize that some things are gone forever. Going back there gave me a feeling that I cannot fully describe. For one moment, it was like yesterday. I was standing where I had stood for so many roll calls.' 'The thing that is hard for people to understand,' he said, 'is that I really was happy here

during the war. Now, the only thing to do is to say 'thank you' to everyone who made this possible. Thank you for all the signs of friendship, thank you for all the kindnesses, thank you for having us. Our dream is to come back. I believe we will do this. But I also know it will not happen like this again.' This is the first time a city has ever brought back a prisoner of war. That is special. Memphis has done it and never again will it be the same."

In 1984, Pelz came back to Memphis in a group of fifteen former P.O.W.s. Five had been prisoners in Memphis while the others had been held in other camps in the Mid-South. Otto Fernholz, a member of Rommel's Africa Corps, cherished the visit:

"I know it's strange, but it's a little bit like coming home. We were treated well here, we made friends and we learned things we have not forgotten. Some say these were lost years. But for most of us, it was an education."

It has been nearly sixty years since German soldiers came to Memphis and Jackson as prisoners of war. Most of the old barracks are gone, and the barbed wire fences and guard towers have been torn down long ago. Yet some still remember the time when German prisoners picked cotton and peaches in Tennessee.

Based on a photograph from *Billy Graham, God's Ambassador,* © 1999 Billy Graham Evangelistic Association, published by Time Life Books.

Billy Graham

When Billy Graham Was in West Tennessee

Several years ago, I wrote an article entitled "Big Crowds in Jackson." The article was inspired by the visit of President Bill Clinton and Vice President Al Gore with their wives, Hillary and Tipper, on August 19, 1996. Clinton was the only president to visit Jackson while he was in office, though several other former presidents who have visited include Andrew Jackson, Lyndon Johnson, Richard Nixon, and Harry Truman. After the article was published, a number of individuals asked about the size of the crowd when Billy Graham came here. It was the first I had heard of his being here. To find the details and date of his visit took five months!

From conversations with a number of individuals, it became obvious that Graham had preached here some time in the early 1950s at Rothrock Stadium.

But fifty years was a long time ago, and no one could remember the exact date. After investigating several sources for definitive information, as a last resort, I sent an e-mail to the Billy Graham Crusade. Their response came back within a few hours, saying he had never come to Jackson! I then sent another e-mail asking when he had been in Memphis. There had been two crusades in Memphis, one in 1951 and one in 1978. The dates for the 1951 crusade were from May 20 to June 20. With this information, I then went to the library and looked at the microfilm copies of *The Jackson Sun* for those dates, and, at last, I found the answer.

Billy Graham did, indeed, preach in Jackson at Rothrock Stadium on Hays Avenue on Friday, June 15, 1951, at the invitation of Dr. Walter F. Jones, president of Union University.

During the thirty-day period when Graham was in Memphis, there were approximately 317,700 people in attendance at the crusade, with 4,868 people coming forward to make decisions of faith. The Memphis meetings were held at E. H. Crump Stadium, having been moved there from the State Fair Arena because of extreme heat and poor acoustics. The campaign was billed as the "Revival under the Stars." Prior to coming to Memphis, the crusade had attracted record-setting crowds at Fort Worth and Shreveport.

On the day he came to Jackson, 5,000 people filled every seat at Rothrock and stood on the sidelines under a hot mid-day sun that disappeared at times as rain threatened. The size of the crowd was remarkable in that there was only a twenty-four-hour advance notice of the event.

Dr. Jones made the welcoming address. Rev. James Canady, president of the Jackson Ministerial Association, introduced dignitaries and officials, and Dr. R. C. Biggs of Union led the opening prayer. The newspaper account described a "respectful motionless quiet" when a young baritone named George Beverly Shea sang his own composition of "I'd Rather Have Jesus" and also "It Is No Secret What God Can Do" written by Stewart Hamblen, a Graham convert. (Crowds would continue to react that way to George Beverly Shea for another fifty years!)

The text of Dr. Graham's sermon was "Communism is not the greatest threat faced by the world, but a lack of Christianity." His message was very timely in that other headlines on the front page of the paper spoke of heavy fighting in Korea. Following his sermon, Dr. Graham and his party were guests at a luncheon at Union. (Remember that Union University was adjacent to and immediately west of Rothrock in 1951.)

At the time that Billy Graham came to Jackson, he was thirty-two years old. Doctors were warning him that he would die within five years if he did not slow down. It has been more than half a century since Billy Graham came to Jackson. He never slowed down, and the doctors were wrong. It would be hard to count or imagine the number of lives he has influenced since that time. And still today in 2004, he continues with crusades in San Diego and Oklahoma City in June.

Jackson has grown and changed since Billy Graham was here. Yet June 15, 1951, remains as one of our brightest days.

*Virginia Military
Institute Shako*

Home for Christmas

November of 1957 seemed to drag on forever. And the first weeks of December seemed even worse. In my imagination, the calendar was stuck. Christmas had never taken this long to arrive. But this year, there was an apparent reason for its belated appearance.

In September of that year, I had entered the Virginia Military Institute (V.M.I.) as a freshman. Nine months of harsh military discipline awaited me, known as "the Rat Line." It is the same system cadets at West Point endure. (Seven of my roommates would quit and go home before the year was out.)

Hazing, physical punishment, and long hours of parades and close order drill made life miserable. Little time was left for studies, and it seemed entirely possible that I would fail freshman chemistry and mathematics. Unshined shoes, unshined brass, and a dirty rifle added demerits and penalty tours at a record rate. If Santa Claus didn't hurry, it looked like I might not make it!

By the first of November, the entire Rat Class (freshmen) were playing Johnny Mathis' Christmas albums in their rooms. Each night as the Corps marched to the dining hall, they sang this song, decreasing the days each night. On the night before Christmas break, it went like this:

"Hark the Herald Angels Shout
One more day till we get out
One more day and we'll be free
Of this place of misery
Grab your ball and grab your chain
Run like Hell for the nearest train
Hark the Herald Angels Shout
One more day till we get out"

At 11:00 on December 18, we were released from barracks with best wishes for a Merry Christmas from the commandant. In civilian clothes for the first time since September, I headed for home. Rain and fog had the Roanoke airport shut down, but thanks to friendly truck drivers and Greyhound, I was home by the next morning.

Looking back through the years, Christmas of 1957 was the best of my life. I was home with family and friends. The

Christmas lights seemed brighter, the packages larger, the holiday food better, and the magic of the season was all around me. And yet forty-six years have passed since that Christmas. The years have dimmed the memories and blended them into recollections of other Christmas seasons. And so, I decided to take a trip back to that Christmas, thanks to microfilmed copies of *The Jackson Sun*. Here is what I found— come and take the trip with me.

On December 19, the weather in Jackson was cloudy with a chance of rain. Though Christmas would not come for another week, I found that Santa Claus arrived about the same time I did. A front-page story in *The Jackson Sun* told of his arrival at the L & N Depot, much to the delight of hundreds of children.

With just a week left before Christmas, last-minute shopping was in full swing.

McCall Hughes advertised men's shirts for three dollars and ninety-five cents. Rosenbloom's had ladies' furs from fifty-five dollars to $850. Holland's advertised Angelique perfume for only two dollars, and calendar towels for 1958 were a dollar. Kisber's advertised a rocket lipstick for a dollar, while a four-mink scarf cost ninety-nine dollars. Nathan's had cashmere coats for eighty-eight dollars. Perel & Lowenstein's had diamond rings from $533 to $1,575. Penney's had men's all-wool suits for twenty-eight dollars.

If you were looking for toys, Farm and Garden had thunder burp guns for three dollars. McGee Ross had a full line of toys. They suggested that you could just call in your order and they would deliver it. Standard Drugs had a free Lionel train set. All you had to do was come to the store and enter a drawing.

The grocery stores had full-page ads as everyone prepared to cook their holiday meals. Turkeys were thirty-five to forty-nine cents per pound depending on the size; a pint tin of select oysters was eighty-nine cents. A five-pound fruitcake was three dollars and ninety-five cents; eggnog was fifty-nine cents a quart, while ham was sixty-three cents a pound. In addition, you could buy any popular brand of cigarettes for two dollars and forty-three cents a carton.

If you did not want to cook your meal at home, the New Southern Hotel advertised "dinner on a dagger," which was a Christmas meal presented on shish kabob. Hiram's Restaurant at 211 West Main had a large ad wishing everyone a Merry Christmas. Joe and all of the employees at Joe's Café sent Christmas greetings, along with a notice that Joe's would close at midnight on Christmas Eve and reopen at midnight on Christmas Day, giving their employees one day off for the holidays!

The sports section of the holiday papers was full of items about bowl games. Tennessee was preparing to play Texas A & M in the Gator Bowl on December 28. Texas A & M was coached by Bear Bryant. Tennessee won three to zero in what would be Bryant's last game before moving on to the University of Alabama! CBS had announced that in April they would begin televising the major league game of the week on Sunday afternoons. There was a great deal of opposition to this, even from Ford Frick, the commissioner of baseball, who thought it was morally incorrect to do so on a Sunday. Eddie Crawford, a football star at Jackson High School and Ole Miss, was slated to start his first game as a defensive halfback for the New York Giants. Pickett Reasonover, the hunting and fishing editor, advised that fishing had been unusually good with all of the mild weather. However, recent cold weather had caused duck hunting to pick up, especially in flooded timber and at Reelfoot Lake, where large concentrations of geese and ducks were located.

The weather was cloudy and mild on both Christmas Eve and Christmas Day, with lows around forty-five and highs of sixty. There was no chance of a white Christmas. The Jaycees held their annual pancake breakfast on Christmas Eve, and the VFW had Christmas lunch for 700 deserving children on Christmas Day. St. Luke's Episcopal Church held its traditional communion and midnight service on Christmas Eve, while the Presbyterians had a 10:00 service on Christmas Day.

On Christmas night, if you wanted a change, there was a tag-team wrestling match with men and women at the National Guard Armory!

It was my best Christmas. And when it was over, even better, I still had a full week before I had to go back to V.M.I.

Tuny (Doris Freeman)

Tuny
"I Am a Lonely Little Petunia in an Onion Patch"

As I write this story, the calendar tells me that it is mid-July. Schools will not reopen for more than a month, and families are on the road for summer vacation, and then, as I lie in bed, the clock radio tells me how many shopping days are left before Christmas Eve!

Perhaps I used to believe that Christmas ran from Thanksgiving to December 25. Not so! Christmas stretches throughout the year, though the holly and tinsel last only for a little while.

Christmas is more than a season. It is a continuation of heightened emotions, sentimentality, and remembrances of loved ones and seasons now gone. Christmas brings out the best in us, and sometimes the reverse. It is a time for unique people who seem to "come onstage" this time of year.

In *Tales of Madison,* I wrote about George Smith. He was my Santa Claus. For me, he will always represent the real spirit of Christmas. As Santa, he was the best of Christmas in the giving of himself to others.

There is another "Christmas person" who comes to mind. Born in 1925, her name was Doris Branch. You may know her as Doris Freeman, but to thousands of people, she is best known as "Cuz" or "Tuny." She is forever dressed as a freckle-faced redhead with pigtails and a blacked-out front tooth. In some ways, she resembles her old friend Minnie Pearl, but she is never a copycat and is different in many ways.

Her costume is designed to make children feel at ease around her—many of them have freckles and missing teeth just like she does. When asked where the nickname Tuny came from, she replies, "I'm a lonely little petunia in an onion patch." Another favorite saying she uses in describing herself is: "When you overdose on maturity, you lose your scooter."

In the early '40s, Tuny's brother-in-law, Aaron Robinson, started a chain of radio stations—the Dixie Broadcasting Network. Tuny went to work for Dixie Broadcasting and began selling radio advertising in Jackson. She was twenty-three years old and the mother of four girls. When her marriage ended in divorce, she became the family's only means of support. Not only did she raise her four daughters, she kept the family together and put all four through school. She was one of Jackson's pioneer broadcasters and the first woman to sell radio advertising.

In 1955, she began doing "The Cousin Tuny Show" on WBBJ television. This show lasted twelve years until 1967. Tuny estimates as many as 7,000 children appeared on that show. With her special appeal to children, you can only speculate how many lives she touched.

For years, Doris was press relations and publicity manager for the Miss Tennessee Pageant. During the annual parade in Atlantic City, she had a special costume. It was a mock old-fashioned swimsuit with a Miss Tennessee rosette. Red, white, and blue high-top shoes, striped socks, and pantaloons completed the outfit. Across the front was a "Miss Hatchie Bottoms" banner.

Doris left television in 1967 and continued on in radio with WDXI in Jackson until 1975. When it was sold, she moved over to another radio station in Jackson, WJAK, until it, too, was sold. In 1980, she became manager and marketing director for Old Hickory Mall in Jackson until it was sold in 1985. She then became marketing and public relations director for General Hospital in Jackson.

In 1963, Doris was selected as Jackson-Madison County Woman of the Year by the Altrusa Club. One of the nominations for the award came from the nurses in the pediatric wing at General Hospital who got the parents of the sick children to sign the nomination.

Doris Freeman wasn't just woman of the year in 1963. She had been Woman of the Year long before that and for decades after. She is one of a kind—a very special cousin. Although she is involved in so many parts of the community, she will always be especially remembered for her work with children. Perhaps you remember her at a Cerebral Palsy or Child Abuse Telethon or for the hours beyond counting spent with "special children" in the hospital.

Christmas is not just a day—it is a spirit of giving without receiving, of care and love for others. Doris Freeman, best known as Cuz, is the epitome of that spirit.

Bibliography

Alexander, Harbert L. R. *History of First Presbyterian Church*. Jackson, Tennessee: Laycook Printing Company, 1998.

Alexander, Harbert L. R. *Tales of Madison*. Franklin, Tennessee: Hillsboro Press, 2002.

Beasley, Gaylon Neil. *True Tales of Tipton*. Covington, Tennessee: The Tipton County Historical Society, 1981.

Busby, Russ. *Billy Graham God's Ambassador, A Lifelong Mission of Giving Hope to the World*. Korea: Dai Nippon Printing Company; Minneapolis, Minnesota: Billy Graham Evangelistic Association; Del Mar, California: Tehabi Books, 1999.

Cartmell, Robert. *Dairies 1849-1915*. Tennessee State Library Association (microfilm), Tennessee Room, Jackson-Madison (Tennessee) County Library.

Cheeney, W. G. *Old Times in West Tennessee*. Memphis, Tennessee: W. G. Cheeney, Printer and Publisher, 1873.

Civil War Centennial Commission. *Tennessee In The Civil War Part I*. Nashville, Tennessee: Civil War Centennial Commission, 1964.

Cobia, Manley F. Jr. *Journey into the Land of Trails, The Story of Davy Crockett's Expedition to the Alamo*. Franklin, Tennessee: Hillsboro Press, 2003.

Crutchfield, James A. *The Natchez Trace, A Pictorial History*. Nashville, Tennessee: Rutledge Hill Press, 1985.

Daniels, Jonathan. *The Devil's Backbone, The Story of the Natchez Trace*. New York, New York: McGraw-Hill Book Company, 1962.

Davis, William C. *Three Roads To The Alamo, The Lives and Fortunes of David Crockett, James Bowie, and William Barret Travis*. New York, New York: Harper-Collins Publishers, 1998.

Freeman, Doris, Cuz. *Tuning in with Cousin Tuny*. Jackson, Tennessee: Main Street Publishing, Inc., 2003.

Gee, Mr. "Randolph Community News," *The Covington Leader,* Covington, Tennessee, 1988-1990.

Israel, Paul. *Edison: A Life of Invention.* New York, New York: John Willey & Sons, Inc., 1998.

Macon, Don M. *Monroe Dunaway Anderson, His Legacy.* Houston, Texas: Texas Medical Center, 1994.

Potter, Jerry O. *The Sultana Tragedy.* Gretna, Louisiana: Pelican Publishing Company, Inc., 1992.

Sodden, Dale E. *The Reverend Mark Matthews, An Activist in the Progressive Era.* Seattle, Washington: University of Washington Press, 2001.

Tabernacle Historical Committee. *The Taylors of Tabernacle, The History of a Family.* Brownsville, Tennessee: Tabernacle Historical Committee, 1957.

Tennessee Historical Commission. *Tennessee Historical Markers.* 8th ed. Nashville, Tennessee: Tennessee Historical Commission, 1996.

Warner, Ezra J. *Generals In Gray.* Baton Rouge, Louisiana: Louisiana State University Press, 1959.

West, Carroll Van ed. *The Tennessee Encyclopedia of History and Culture.* Nashville, Tennessee: Rutledge Hill Press, 1998.

Williams, Edward F. III. *Early Memphis and Its River Rivals: Fulton, Randolph and Fort Pickering.* Reprinted from the West Tennessee Historical Society Papers. Vol XXII. 1968.

Williams, Emma Inman. *Historic Madison.* 3rd ed. Kingsport, Tennessee: Arcata Graphics, 1986.

Williams, Emma Inman, Marion B. Smothers, and Mitch Carter. *Jackson and Madison County: A Pictorial History.* Norfolk, Virginia: The Donning Company, 1988.

Wills, Ridley II. *The History of Belle Meade: Mansion, Plantation and Stud.* Nashville, Tennessee: Vanderbilt University Press, 1991.

Index

(Bold folios indicate illustrations.)

Index

To order additional copies of
Old Trails and Tales of Tennessee
at $29.95 plus $6.00 postage, handling,
and sales tax ($35.95 total per copy),
send checks payable to
Harbert Alexander
1723 North Highland Avenue
Jackson, Tennessee 38301

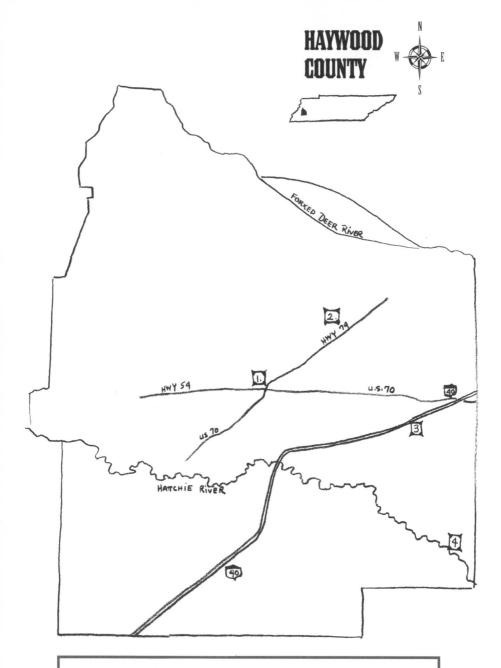

HAYWOOD COUNTY

FORKED DEER RIVER

HWY 79

HWY 54

U.S. 70

US 70

HATCHIE RIVER

40

1) Halliburton Home, Brownsville
2) Tabernacle Campground and
   Taylor Cemetery
3) Woodland Baptist Church
*4) Estanaula Landing
*5) Denmark Presbyterian Church

*6) Battle of Britton Lane
*7) Murrell Home
8) German P.O.W. Camp
9) Jackson
*10) Boone Tree
*11) Carroll Station